KATRINE MARÇAL

Who Cooked Adam Smith's Dinner?

A Story About Women and Economics

Translated from the Swedish by Saskia Vogel

Portobello
BOOKS

Published by Portobello Books 2015
Portobello Books
12 Addison Avenue
London
W11 4QR

A CIP catalogue record for this book is available from the British Library

ISBN 978 1 84627 564 7
eISBN 978 1 84627 565 4

www.portobellobooks.com

Typeset by Avon DataSet Ltd, Bidford on Avon, Warwickshire
Printed and bound by CPI Group (UK) Ltd, Croydon, CR0 4YY

MIX
Paper from
responsible sources
FSC® C020471

'Economics is about money and why it is good'

Woody Allen

CONTENTS

DISCLAIMER   ix

PROLOGUE   1

CHAPTER ONE
*In which we climb into the world of economics and ask
ourselves who Adam Smith's mother was*   7

CHAPTER TWO
*In which we are introduced to economic man and
realize that he is incredibly seductive*   18

CHAPTER THREE
*In which it becomes apparent that economic man is
not a woman*   29

CHAPTER FOUR
*In which we see that our pact with economic man isn't
turning out as we had expected*   42

CHAPTER FIVE
In which we add women and stir   56

CHAPTER SIX
In which Las Vegas and Wall Street merge   68

CHAPTER SEVEN
In which the global economy goes to hell   80

CHAPTER EIGHT
In which we see that men are also not like economic man   94

CHAPTER NINE
*In which economic incentives aren't shown to be as
uncomplicated as we might think*   105

CHAPTER TEN
*In which we see that you aren't selfish just because you
want more money*   116

CHAPTER ELEVEN
In which we see that a negative number is still zero   126

CHAPTER TWELVE
In which we all become entrepreneurs   139

CHAPTER THIRTEEN
In which we see that the uterus isn't a space capsule   148

CHAPTER FOURTEEN
*In which we discover economic man's unforeseen depths
and fears*   157

CHAPTER FIFTEEN
*In which we see that the greatest story of our time only
has one sex*   170

CHAPTER SIXTEEN
*In which we will see that every society suffers in line
with its bullshit. And we say goodbye.*   179

EPILOGUE   190
NOTES   198
BIBLIOGRAPHY   217
CREDITS   228
INDEX OF PERSONS   229

DISCLAIMER

The protagonist in this book is fictional and bears little resemblance to persons living or dead. The reality depicted doesn't exist, really. The economic theories that the protagonist is derived from have very little to do with reality. Any similarities between readers and the book's protagonist are coincidental.

This is because you want to be like him. And not because you are.

PROLOGUE

Feminism has always been about economics. Virginia Woolf wanted a room of her own, and that costs money.

In the late nineteenth and early twentieth centuries women joined together to demand the right of inheritance, the right of ownership, the right to start their own companies, the right to borrow money, the right to employment, equal pay for equal work and the option to support themselves so that they didn't need to marry for money, and could instead marry for love.

Feminism continues to be about money.

Feminism's aim for the past decades has been to take money and privilege from men in exchange for less quantifiable things like 'the right to cry in public'.

Or at least that's how some people put it.

More than six years have passed since 15 September 2008, the day the American investment bank Lehman Brothers filed for bankruptcy. Within a few weeks banks and insurance companies around the world followed suit. Millions of people lost their jobs and their savings. Families were forced to give up their houses, governments fell, the markets shook. Panic swept from one part of the economy to the next and from one country to another as a system that couldn't stand up any more stumbled forward.

We watched in wonder.

If everyone just works, pays their taxes and keeps quiet, everything will sort itself out.

That's what we'd been taught.

But that was false.

After the crisis, one international conference was held after another. Book upon book was written about what had gone wrong and what needed to be done. Suddenly, everyone seemed to be criticizing capitalism, from Conservative politicians to the Pope in Rome. It was said that this crisis was a paradigm shift, that everything would now be different. The global financial system needed to change. New values would have to dominate the economy. We read about greed, about global imbalances and about income inequality. We heard ad nauseam that the Chinese word for 'crisis' was made up of two characters, one meaning 'danger', the other 'possibility'.

(Which isn't correct, by the way.)

Six years later the financial sector has recovered. Profits, salaries, dividends and bonuses are back to what they once were.

The economic order and the economic story that so many thought would disappear with the crisis proved to be stubborn. Intellectually robust. The question is, why? There are many answers. This book aims to give you one perspective on the matter: that of sex.

And not in the way you might think.

If Lehman Brothers had been Lehman Sisters, the financial crisis would have turned out differently, said Christine Lagarde in 2010, when she was still France's Minister of Finance.

Presumably not entirely seriously.

Audur Capital, an Icelandic private equity fund entirely

run by women, was the only fund of its kind that made it through the crisis without so much as a scratch, she pointed out. And there are studies that show that men with higher testosterone levels are more prone to taking risks. Excessive risk-taking is what causes banks to capsize and financial crises to occur, so does this mean that men are too hormonal to run the economy?

There are other studies that show that women are at least as prone to taking risks as men, but only when they are in the middle of their menstrual cycles. Is the problem with male bankers that they are like ovulating women? What is the connection between the business cycle and the menstrual cycle?

Further studies note that girls in all-girls schools are just as eager as boys to take risks. Girls in mixed schools, on the other hand, are more cautious. In other words, norms and ideas about what your sex is in relation to the so-called opposite sex seem to matter.

At least when the opposite sex is present.

We can joke about these things, or take them seriously, but one fact remains: Lehman Brothers would never have been Lehman Sisters. A world where women dominated Wall Street would have had to be so completely different from the actual world that to describe it wouldn't tell us anything about the actual world. Thousands of years of history would need to be rewritten in order to lead up to the hypothetical moment that an investment bank named Lehman Sisters could handle its over-exposure to an overheated American housing market.

The thought experiment is meaningless.

You can't just switch out 'brothers' for 'sisters'.

The story of women and economics is much bigger than that.

Feminism is a tradition of thought and political action that goes back more than two hundred years. It is one of the great democratic political movements of our time, no matter what you think about its conclusions. And feminism has also accounted for what is probably the largest systemic economic shift of the last century.

Some would say ever.

'Women went to work in the 1960s': that's how this story is usually told.

But it's not true. Women didn't 'go to work' in the 1960s or during the Second World War.

Women have always worked.

What has happened in the last decades is that women have changed jobs.

From working in the home, they've taken positions out on the market and started to take payment for their labour.

From having worked as nurses, carers, teachers and secretaries they have started competing with men as doctors, lawyers and marine biologists.

This represents a gigantic social and economic shift: half of the population has moved the majority of its work from the home to the market.

We went from one economic system to another, without really being aware of it.

At the same time, family life has been transformed.

As recently as 1950 American women on average gave birth to four children each. Today that number is down to two.

In Great Britain and the USA, women's family patterns

have arranged themselves in accordance with their level of education. Well-educated women have fewer children, and they have them later in life. Women with less education have more children, and they have them a lot younger.

In the media, both of these groups are depicted as caricatures.

The career woman with the screaming baby in her briefcase, she who waited until she turned forty to push out her offspring, and now she doesn't even have time to take care of it.

She is selfish, irresponsible and a bad woman.

The young working-class mother sitting in her council flat, living off benefits and without a man in her life.

She is also selfish, also irresponsible and also a bad woman.

The debate about the colossal economic shift that we have gone through often starts and ends here: in opinions about how individual women, or caricatures of these women, should live their lives.

In Scandinavia, where society invests enormous sums in childcare and paid parental leave, a woman's family pattern is more unified, no matter what her level of education is. Generally she gives birth to more children as well. But even in these world-renowned welfare states women earn less than men and the number of women in senior management positions in business is small compared with many other countries.

Somewhere there is an equation that no one has managed to solve.

Maybe we don't even have the language to talk about it yet, but it is without doubt an economic equation.

Many people are afraid of economics. Its words, its authority,

its rituals and its apparently all-encompassing incompre-
hensibility. The period that led up to the great financial crisis
was a time when we were asked to hand the economy over
to the experts. It was said that they had solved the issues for
us and we weren't competent enough to understand their
solution. It was a period when central bankers could become
celebrities and be named 'Man of the Year' by *Time* magazine
for cutting interest rates to save western civilization.

That era has passed.

This is a story about being seduced. It's about how
insidiously a certain view of economics has crawled under our
skin. How it has been allowed to dominate other values, not
just in the global economy, but in our own lives. It's about men
and women and about how when we make toys real, they gain
power over us.

To tie it all together, we need to start at the beginning.

CHAPTER ONE

In which we climb into the world of economics and
ask ourselves who Adam Smith's mother was

How do you get your dinner? That's the fundamental question of economics. It seems simple, but it is extremely complicated.

Most of us produce only a small percentage of what we consume every day. We buy the rest. The bread sits on the shelf in the store, and electricity flows through the wires when we turn on the lamp. But two loaves of bread and one kilowatt of electricity require the coordinated activity of thousands of people around the world.

The farmer who cultivates the wheat that is sold to the bread factory. The company that sells the bags to package bread. The bread factory that sells bread to the supermarket and the supermarket that sells bread to you. This all needs to happen so the bread will be there on the shelf any given Tuesday – and then there are the people who sell tools to the farmers, transport the groceries to the store, maintain the vehicles, clean the supermarkets and unpack the goods.

This whole process must take place approximately on time, in approximately the right order and enough times so that the shelves in the bakery aren't empty. This must happen not only for every loaf of bread, but also for every book, Barbie doll, bomb, balloon and anything else we can think of buying and selling. Modern economies are intricate things.

And so the economists ponder: what keeps it all together?

Economics has been described as the science of how you conserve love. The basic idea goes: love is scarce. It's difficult to love your neighbour, not to mention your neighbour's neighbour. Therefore we must conserve our love and not use it up unnecessarily. If we fuel our society with it, there won't be any left over for our private lives. Love is hard to find – and even harder to maintain. That's why economists determined that we needed to organize society around something else.

Why not use self-interest instead? That seems to be available in surplus.

In 1776 Adam Smith, the father of political economy, wrote the words that shaped our modern understanding of economics:

'It is not from the benevolence of the butcher, the brewer, or the baker, that we expect our dinner, but from their regard to their own interest.'

Smith's idea was that the butcher works in order to have satisfied customers and therefore money. Not to be nice. The baker bakes and the brewer brews not because they want to make people happy but to turn a profit. If the bread and the beer are good, people will buy them. That is why bakers and brewers produce their goods. Not because they actually care that people get good bread and tasty beer. That's not the driving force. The driving force is self-interest.

You can trust self-interest. Self-interest is inexhaustible.

Love, on the other hand. Love is scarce. There isn't enough

of it to go around in society; it should be conserved in a tin intended for personal use. Otherwise, everything would spoil.

'What's 100 metres long, moves at a snail's pace and lives only on cabbage?'

Answer: 'The queue for a bakery in the Soviet Union.'

We don't want things to be like they were in the Soviet Union.

Adam Smith told us the story of why free markets were the best way to create an efficient economy. His ideas about freedom and autonomy were revolutionary and radical. Away with duties and regulations. When the market is allowed to operate freely the economy will run like clockwork, ticking away on an unlimited supply of self-interest, he reasoned. With everyone working to serve themselves, everyone will have access to the goods they need. The bread is there on the shelf, electricity runs through the wires. And you get your dinner.

The self-interest of one and all ensures that the whole comes together. Without anyone actually having to think about the whole. It's magic. And this has become one of the most celebrated stories of our time.

In the early days of economics, it was clear that selfishness made the world turn.

'The first principle of economics is that every agent is actuated only by self-interest,' economists wrote at the end of the 1800s. The modern economy was built on 'the granite of self-interest', and it is a wonder for us all to admire.

Economics wasn't about money. From the beginning it was about how we view people. Essentially, economics was a history of how we behave in order to profit from any given situation. In every situation. No matter what the consequences.

This is still the starting point of standard economic theories. When we speak colloquially about 'thinking like an economist' this is what we mean: people do what they do because it benefits them. It is perhaps not the most flattering picture of mankind. But it is the most accurate. And, we're told, if you want to get anything done you might as well be realistic. Morality represents the way we would like the world to work, economists tell us how it actually does work. At least, that's what they themselves say.

And we don't need to know any more than that. This is how we move through life. And thanks to this, society is held together. As if by an invisible hand. That is the great paradox.

And as we all know, God always speaks to us in paradoxes.

'The invisible hand' is the best-known expression in economics. Adam Smith coined the term, but it's the economists since him who popularized it. The invisible hand touches everything, guides everything, is in everything, decides everything – but you can neither see nor feel it. It doesn't intervene from above, outside, point and move things around. It arises in and between the actions and choices of individuals. It is the hand that drives the system – from within. The concept was more central to later economists than it was for Adam Smith himself. The father of political economy mentions the term only once in *The Wealth of Nations*, but nowadays it is often considered the foundation of economics and its singular universe.

*

A century before Adam Smith wrote about the invisible hand, the Englishman Isaac Newton published his work *Philosophiae Naturalis Principia Mathematica*.

Astronomer, mathematician, natural scientist and alchemist, Newton explained the forces that kept the moon on its course. He calculated the movements of planets, gravity's pull and why apples plummet to the ground – all guided by the same gravity that carries the heavenly bodies in its arms.

Newton gave us modern science and a whole new view of existence.

In his time, mathematics was considered a divine language. It was through mathematics that God had made 'the book of nature' intelligible to mankind. God gave us mathematics so that we could understand his creation. Newton's findings intoxicated the whole world.

Perhaps most of all, Adam Smith and the burgeoning political economy.

The laws of the solar system that previously only God had known could suddenly be read using scientific method. The view of the world changed. From one where God intervened, had opinions, smote, parted oceans, moved mountains and personally opened millions of flowers every day. To one where God was absent and the universe was a clock that he had created and wound up, but that now ticked of its own accord.

The world became an apparatus, a bloody great automaton, a gigantic performance where the various parts whirred as if in a machine. The intellectuals of the time increasingly believed that you could explain everything else the same way Newton explained the movement of the planets. Isaac Newton had revealed the laws of nature – and with them God's true plan for the world.

Surely the same approach should be able to reveal the laws of society, thought Adam Smith, and with them God's true plan for mankind.

If there was a mechanism in nature, there should be a mechanism in society.

If there were laws that heavenly bodies moved in accordance with, there should be laws that human bodies moved in accordance with.

And they should be able to be expressed scientifically.

If only we could understand these laws, we could adapt society to flow with them. We would be able to live in harmony with the true plan. Swim *with* the forces, not *against* them, and, moreover, comprehend everything. Society could be frictionless as clockwork, ticking in precisely the way that was best for us.

This was the task that Adam Smith and economics took on. And it was hardly a small task. How do we achieve natural harmony?

The force that was assumed to fill the same function in society as gravity did in the solar system – that was self-interest.

'I can calculate the motion of heavenly bodies but not the madness of people,' said Newton himself. But no one cared. Adam Smith seemed to have revealed God's true plan for the world: a system of natural liberty portrayed as a perfect mirror image of Newtonian physics.

If you want to understand something – pick it apart. This was Newton's methodology. Split the whole into smaller pieces. If you still can't understand it – take it apart again.

Break it into even smaller pieces. And so on. Finally, you'll arrive at the smallest possible piece that the whole can be divided into. The fundamental Lego block that everything else is made up of. The elementary particle. The atom. The smallest component. Then you can study it. If you can understand this piece – you can understand everything.

Changes in the whole do not occur because the particles themselves are changing; the particles are always independent of what they are participating in. Every shift is just a new pattern that they have arranged themselves in. Their movements are driven by the laws of nature. And the world is as logical as clockwork.

Economists tried to replicate this trick. If you want to understand the economy – pick it apart. Split up each complex coordinated process that is needed for steak to be at the butcher's any given Tuesday. If you still don't understand it, pick it apart again. Break it into even smaller bits. When the pieces became smaller and smaller, economists found the smallest possible component that they believed the whole could be divided into. And they called this the 'individual'.

If you understand the individual, you understand everything, they thought. In the same way that the physics of the time was devoted to indivisible atoms, economics was devoted to autonomous individuals. Society is simply the sum of these individuals. If the economy changes, it's not because the individual has changed – his identity is always unaffected by others. But he does make choices. Every change is just a new pattern that he has arranged himself in. New choices that he has made in relation to others. They never meet, but they interact. Like billiard balls. The consciousness of the individual, that no one but the individual himself has a say over, will remain forever unchanged.

And the rest is silence.

Adam Smith's greatest achievement lay in that he, from the start, successfully mapped the burgeoning discipline of economics onto the world view of physics. Logical, rational and predictable. That's how physics seemed to be in this period. This was before time and space melted together into indivisible spacetime. Before the universe divided itself at every occasion of measurement into as many worlds as the number of possible outcomes at the time of measurement. But economists have never cared much about modern physics. They are still staring at the stars in Newton's sky.

'What really interests me is whether God had any choice in the creation of the world,' Albert Einstein, the father of modern physics, asked himself in the early twentieth century. Is there an unknown alternative to Newton's laws of physics? Another way of doing things? Contemporary economists rarely thought along these lines. They were sure of themselves. Economic theory is 'a body of generalization whose substantial accuracy and importance are open to question only by the ignorant or the perverse,' wrote the British economist Lionel Robbins in 1945. The very point is that there is no alternative. The market lived in human nature. And economists studied the market, and so they studied people.

At one time kings hired court counsellors who interpreted patterns apparent in the intestines of dead animals. They studied their colours and shapes to inform their ruler of how the gods could be expected to react to one political decision or another. In pre-historic Italy, the Etruscans divided the outer layers of a sheep's liver into sixteen separate pieces. But the world has evolved since then. Today, these counsellors' roles have been taken over by economists. With more or less accuracy, they try to prophesy how the market will react to one decision or another that the politicians are considering.

Many of us want to live in a market economy, but not in a market society. We have been taught that we must take the one with the other. Fidel Castro says that the only thing worse than being exploited by multinational capitalism is not being exploited by multinational capitalism. He may be right. 'There is no alternative,' said Margaret Thatcher. Capitalism seemed (at least until the financial crisis of 2008) to have succeeded where all the great world religions had failed: uniting humanity in a single fellowship. The global market.

The market can decide what iron and silver should cost, what people's needs are, how much nannies, pilots and CEOs should earn. What she should pay for a lipstick, for a lawn mower and to have her uterus surgically removed. The market dictates what it is worth for an investment bank to crash straight into the taxpayers' reserves (70 million dollars a year). And what it is worth to hold an eighty-seven-year-old woman's anxious hand as she takes her last 700 breaths in a Scandinavian welfare state (ninety-six krona – around eight pounds – an hour).

When Adam Smith got his dinner, he didn't think it was because the butcher and baker liked him – he thought it was that their interests were served through trade. It was self-interest that put dinner on the table for Adam Smith.

Or, was it? Who actually prepared that steak?

Adam Smith never married. The father of economics lived with his mother for most of his life. She tended to the house and a cousin handled Adam Smith's finances. When Adam Smith was appointed as a commissioner of customs in Edinburgh, his mother moved with him. Her entire life, she took care of her son, and she is the part of the answer to the question of how we get our dinner that Adam Smith omits.

For the butcher, the baker and the brewer to be able to go to work, at the time Adam Smith was writing, their wives, mothers or sisters had to spend hour after hour, day after day minding the children, cleaning the house, cooking the food, washing the clothes, drying tears and squabbling with the neighbours. However you look at the market, it is always built on another economy. An economy that we rarely discuss.

The eleven-year-old girl who walks fifteen kilometres every morning to gather wood for her family plays a big part in her country's ability to develop economically. But her work isn't acknowledged. The girl is invisible in economic statistics. In the GDP calculation, which measures the total economic activity in a country, she isn't counted. What she does is not considered important for the economy. Or for growth. Giving birth to babies, raising children, cultivating a garden, cooking food for her siblings, milking the family cow, making clothes for her relatives or taking care of Adam Smith so he can write *The Wealth of Nations*. None of this is counted as 'productive activity' in the standard economic models.

Beyond the reach of the invisible hand there is the invisible sex.

The French author and feminist Simone de Beauvoir described woman as 'the second sex'. It's the man who comes first. It's the man who counts. He defines the world and woman is 'the other', everything he is not but also that which he is dependent on so he can be who he is.

Be the one who counts.

In the same way that there is a 'second sex', there is a 'second economy'. The work that is traditionally carried out by men is what counts. It defines the economic world view. Women's work is 'the other'. Everything that he doesn't do but that he is dependent on so he can do what he does.

Do the things that count.

Adam Smith only succeeded in answering half of the fundamental question of economics. He didn't get his dinner only because the tradesmen served their own self-interests through trade. Adam Smith got his dinner because his mother made sure it was on the table every evening.

Today it is sometimes pointed out that the economy isn't just built with an 'invisible hand', it is also built with an 'invisible heart'. But perhaps this is an over-idealized picture of the tasks that society has historically assigned to women. We don't know why Adam Smith's mother took care of her son.

We just know that she did.

CHAPTER TWO

*In which we are introduced to economic man and
realize that he is incredibly seductive*

A. A. Milne, the author of the *Winnie the Pooh* books, noted
that children especially were fascinated by stories of desert
islands. Stories of being stranded in a new and isolated world
sparked their imagination in a singular way.

Milne thought that it was because the isolated island
provided the child with the most effective escape from real life.
No mum, no dad, no siblings; no family obligations, duties,
conflicts or power struggles. A whole new world. Cleaner and
simpler. You are free and alone, yours are the only footsteps in
the sand.

This is a world in which the child itself can be the master,
usurp the throne and proclaim itself the sun god.

You could say that economists are a bit like children. Many
of them are completely obsessed with Robinson Crusoe. Most
students of economics will have heard their professor retell the
story of Daniel Defoe's 1719 novel in some way. You might
wonder what a story about a white, racist man who lives alone
on an island for twenty-six years before becoming friends with

a 'savage' could possibly tell us about modern-day economies.

But then you haven't understood the crux of economics.

Daniel Defoe's shipwrecked hero has become the ultimate blueprint for what economists call economic man. Crusoe is stranded on a desert island without social codes or laws. No one inhibits him and he has carte blanche to act out of self-interest. On Crusoe's island the self-interest that drives the economy is separate from other considerations, and therefore the story becomes a didactic tool for economists.

When we participate in the market, we're all assumed to be anonymous. That's why the market can set us free. It doesn't matter who you are. Personal traits and emotional ties don't have a place here. The only thing that matters is your ability to pay. The choices people make are free and independent, we have no history or context, we are isolated islands in an otherwise empty sea. No one judges us and nothing binds us or holds us back. The only limitations are technical: the finite hours of the day and our natural resources. Robinson Crusoe is free and his relationships with other people are chiefly about what they can do for him.

He doesn't act out of ill will, that's simply not rational – as far as reason is constructed in the story.

In the novel, Robinson Crusoe is born in York, England. Dad is a merchant and Robinson has two older brothers. One dies in a war and the other just disappears. Robinson studies law but isn't enticed by the comforts of English middle-class life. Instead, he boards a ship bound for Africa. After several journeys, he finally lands in Brazil. There, he founds what will eventually become a very successful plantation. Robinson Crusoe grows rich. But Robinson Crusoe wants to be even richer. Ships are heading to Africa to collect slaves, and he climbs aboard one. On the last leg of its journey, the vessel he's travelling on sinks, and Robinson alone is cast upon a nearby desert isle.

Here the adventure begins.

Robinson spends many years in isolation with only a few animals for company. 'Savages' and cannibals wreak havoc on the beaches. In his log book, in parallel columns, he lists not only money and materials, but also luck and misfortune.

Yes, it is true he's on a desert island – but he's alive.

He might be isolated from others – but he isn't starving.

He might not have any clothes – but the weather is good.

Robinson logically calculates the benefits of each situation. And he is rather happy. Free from demands, envy and pride. Free of other people. Triumphantly, he writes that he can do exactly as he pleases. He can call himself emperor or king of the entire island. What joy! Free from distractions and carnal desires, he instead focuses on ownership and control. The island is his to conquer and nature is there for him to govern.

Robinson Crusoe is usually retold as a story about the inventiveness and ingenuity of the individual. Robinson harvests corn, makes pots and milks goats. He makes candles out of goat tallow, and twines wicks made of dried nettles. But it's not just Robinson's ingenuity that builds up this little one-man society. In fact, he takes thirteen trips to the wrecked ship to retrieve materials and tools. He uses these to take command of nature and eventually of other people.

The tools and materials are made by others, even if they are far away. And Robinson is completely dependent on their labour.

During his twenty-sixth year on the island Robinson runs into a native. He saves him from the cannibals and christens him after the day of the week on which they met. Friday's gratitude knows no bounds. He has a child-like love for Robinson and works for him like a slave. Friday, who is a cannibal himself, has a certain longing for human flesh, but changes his diet out of consideration for Robinson.

They spend the next three years together, as described by the novel's author, 'perfectly and completely happy'. In the end, they are rescued and travel back to Europe.

When they arrive in Lisbon, Robinson discovers he is incredibly well-off. The plantation in Brazil has been taken care of by his workers and has turned great profits in the years that he was gone. Robinson sells his shares, marries and has three children. Then his wife dies. This series of events – marriage, childbirth and death – is described in a single sentence in the novel.

And Crusoe goes to sea again.

The Irish writer James Joyce described Robinson as the embodiment of 'the manly independence; the unconscious cruelty; the persistence; the slow yet efficient intelligence; the sexual apathy … the calculating taciturnity.'

Robinson Crusoe is isolated, and economists like to isolate people. A shipwrecked Robinson on a desert island makes it possible to contemplate how people would act if there weren't a world around them. Most standard economic models are based on precisely this. *Ceteris paribus*, economics professors sermonize. 'All other things being equal or constant.' You have to isolate a single variable within an economic model that encompasses several variables – otherwise it won't work. Clever economists have always been aware of the flaw in this approach, but it continues to form the basis of 'thinking like an economist'. One has to simplify the world to be able to predict it, and so one has chosen, in the spirit of Adam Smith, to simplify it in precisely this way.

In the novel, Robinson Crusoe quickly creates an economy. He trades and buys even though there isn't any money on the island – goods are valued according to demand.

Another story about shipwrecked men is often used by economists to illustrate the principle that value is determined by demand.

Imagine two men on a desert island: the one has a sack of rice and the other has 200 golden bracelets. At home on the mainland one golden bracelet could have bought a sack of rice, but now, the two men aren't on the mainland. The men are shipwrecked, and the value of the goods has changed.

The man with the rice suddenly can ask for all of the golden bracelets in exchange for just one portion. He may even refuse to trade at all. Because what would he do with a golden bracelet on a desert island? Economists love to tell this kind of story; they nod and think they've revealed something profound about how mankind functions.

These stories never allow for the possibility that two people abandoned on a desert island would start talking to each other, that they might be feeling lonely. Scared. Might need each other. After conversing for a while, they'd realize that they both had hated spinach when they were children and had uncles who were alcoholics. After discussing this for a while, they'd probably share the rice.

That we humans can react in this way, doesn't that have economic importance?

The men in the economists' story are not first and foremost stranded on an island. They are stranded in themselves. Alone. Isolated. Unreachable. Incapable of interacting with each other in any way but through trade and competition. Incapable of relating to the surrounding world as anything but a set of goods. Everything must be bought, traded and sold for the largest profit possible.

Robinson Crusoe is first and foremost an example of economic man. Economists have dubbed him *Homo economicus*, and he provides the basis for economic theories as we know them. Economics decided it was the individual that one should study, and therefore one needed to create a simplified story of how this individual acted. Thus was born the model of human behaviour that has defined economic thought since then.

And moreover: this individual is an incredibly seductive person.

Those who study economics learn a story of a man who goes out into the world to maximize his profits using the conditions and hurdles he encounters along the way. He is said to be a universal, if simplified, description of what a person is. For woman as for man, for rich as for poor, irrespective of culture or religion, legs or arms. Economic man claims to represent the pure economic consciousness that resides in each of us. That which formulates desires and then tries to satisfy them.

He is rational and driven by reason, he doesn't do anything he isn't forced to, and if he does anything, he'll do it for pleasure or to avoid pain. He will always take all he can and do everything he can to overcome, circumvent and ultimately destroy those who stand in his way.

Economists' standard models say that this person, at the core, is who we are. In any case, it's the part of ourselves that is economically relevant. And so it's this part of us that economists should study. Our most fundamental trait is that we want an unlimited number of things. Everything. Now. Immediately. People's unlimited desires are limited only by the world's scarce resources and because everyone else wants things too. Everything. Now. Immediately. And when we can't have all we want, then we have to choose. Out of scarcity, choice is born.

Choice means lost opportunities. Lost gains that might have come from the alternatives one hasn't chosen. If you choose to go in one direction, you can't also choose the other.

Economic man has his preferences.

If he prefers tulips to roses and roses to ox-eye daisies, it means that he also prefers tulips to ox-eye daisies. And he is always rational – he always chooses the least costly path to reach his goal.

We think of what we want and then we act to get it. Calculating the shortest possible distance between point A and point B. As much as possible, as cheap as possible. This is what it's all about. You decide what you want to have and in which order. I decide what I want to have and in which order. Then we try to get it. Ready, set, go. Then life begins. And ends, for that matter. Buy low, sell high.

The great advantage of economic man is that he's predictable. That's why you can express all the problems he encounters through elegant mathematics. If people are like him, people can be accounted for. There is only self-interest, and from a dead universe we can establish the natural laws that govern society.

Just like Robinson Crusoe, economic man was a modern entrepreneur who freed himself from old, irrational oppressions. Just like Robinson Crusoe, he could take care of himself, there was no king or emperor who could tell him what to do. He was his own king or emperor, he was free and no one owned him. This was the new person that economics carried into the new age.

Economic man determined his life and let others determine theirs. He was highly capable. Simply because he was human. His superior faculties of reason made him the master of his own world, not another's servant or subordinate. He was free. And in every situation, he could survey all the possible alternatives with lightning speed and make the best possible decision. He moved through an environment full of choices like a world-class chess player. That's human nature, said economists in the 1800s. And he showed tolerance: economic man judged people not on where they came from, but on where they were going. He was also curious and open to change. He always wanted to be even better off. Have more. See more. Experience more.

Work has no intrinsic value, thinks economic man, but if you're going to get anywhere, you have to do it. He makes goals, fights to achieve them, ticks them off and moves on. He never gets caught up in what has been; he only looks ahead. If he wants you, he'll do everything he can to get you. Lie, steal, fight and sell everything he has. He is alone, but his solitude is lusty. He does everything he can to satisfy his desires. But he'd rather negotiate and bargain than use violence. Not everyone can suckle at the teat simultaneously. The world's resources are limited. And he admires those who succeed. It's about pleasure. Life. To wrap your hands around something you've worked hard for and to be able to say, 'This is mine.'

At the end of the movie, he rides off into the sunset alone.

Emotion, altruism, thoughtfulness, solidarity are not part of his character in the standard economic theories. Economic man can express a preference for solidarity or for a certain feeling, but it's a preference – just like he may prefer apples to pears. He requests emotions – wants to have that experience. But it's never part of him. For economic man there's no childhood, no dependencies and no society that affect him. He remembers his own birth. It was the same as anything else.

Rational, selfish and divorced from his environment. Alone on an island or alone in society. It doesn't matter. There is no society, only a mass of individuals.

Economics became the science of 'conserving love'. Society was held together by self-interest. From Adam Smith's invisible hand was born an economic man. Love was then reserved for the private sphere. It was important to keep it outside.

Otherwise the honey would run out.

Bernard de Mandeville, a Dutch doctor practising in England, published his famous book *The Fable of the Bees* in 1714. Satirically, he writes that when each and every bee pursues its self-interest at the same time, then they find out what's best for the hive. Self-interest serves the greater good, as long as the bees can carry on uninterrupted. If one interferes, there won't be any honey. Vanity, envy and greed paradoxically increase the collective happiness in the hive. These low feelings make the bees work even harder. We get economic growth and ever-flowing honey. *Greed is good*. And in the end, it's self-interest that we can depend on.

If everyone would simply be selfish, then in a magical way this selfishness will be transformed into what is best for the whole. It's the same story Smith told. The 'invisible hand' of the economy can transform our egoism and greed into harmony and balance. It is a story that holds its own against the power of the deepest mysteries of the Catholic Church to invest us with meaning and give us absolution. Through your greed and your egoism you will be reconciled with other people.

'America makes no sense without a deeply held faith – and I don't care what it is,' said President Dwight D. Eisenhower.

Over the centuries the idea that the economy was guided by an invisible hand developed into the myth that the market could almost bring about the end of history. Make money, not war, as if the two had nothing to do with each other. It was supposed that when our economic interests became ever more interconnected, the primitive conflicts of the past wouldn't be necessary any more. You don't shoot your cousin because he's Muslim if you have shared economic interests. You don't kill your neighbour because your daughter has slept with him if your business depends on him.

The invisible hand prevents you.

The bloody events of the twentieth century have shown that people really aren't that simple. But it's a good story. And few interrogate a good story.

In any case, not in depth and of our own volition.

The market's machinery was supposed to be able to create world peace and happiness for all from something as simple as our normal, base feelings. And it's no wonder we were seduced. Exploitation wasn't personal any more. The woman who breaks her back for six dollars an hour doesn't do so because someone is evil or has sentenced her to it. No one is guilty, no one is responsible. It's the economy, stupid. And economics is unavoidable. It's in your nature. Actually, it is your essence.

Because we are all like economic man.

CHAPTER THREE

*In which it becomes apparent that economic man is
not a woman*

Men have always been allowed to act out of self-interest – as in economics, so in sex. For women, this freedom has been taboo.

If not flat-out forbidden.

Woman has been assigned the task of caring for others, not of maximizing her own gain. Society has told her that she cannot be rational because childbirth and menstruation tie her to the body, and the body has been identified as the opposite of reason.

In women, lust and greed has always been criticized more harshly than it has in men. It has been viewed as something threatening, destructive, dangerous and unnatural. 'People call me a feminist whenever I express sentiments that differentiate me from a doormat or a prostitute,' wrote Rebecca West. Women have never been allowed to be as selfish as men.

And if economics is the science of self-interest, how does woman fit in?

The answer is that man has been allowed to stand for self-interest and woman has stood for the fragile love that must be conserved. By being excluded.

*

29

Even though the word 'economy' comes from the Greek *oikos*, which means home, economists have long been uninterested in what exactly happens at home. Woman's self-sacrificing nature was said to tie her to the private sphere, and thus she was not economically relevant.

Activities like raising children, cleaning, washing or ironing for her family – these don't create tangible goods that can be bought, traded or sold. So they also didn't contribute to prosperity, thought economists in the 1800s. Prosperity was everything that could be transported, that had a limited supply, and that either directly or indirectly gave pleasure or prevented pain.

This definition meant that everything that women were expected to dedicate themselves to went unseen.

The fruits of male labour could be stacked in piles and measured in money. The results of women's work were intangible. Dust that is swept away collects again. Mouths that have been fed grow hungry. Children who sleep, wake. And after lunch it's time to do the dishes. After the dishes comes dinner. And more dirty dishes.

Housework is cyclical in nature. Therefore, women's work wasn't an 'economic activity'. What she did was just a logical extension of her fair, loving nature. She would always carry out this work, and so it wasn't anything that one needed to spend time quantifying. It came from a logic other than the economic.

Out of the feminine. And other.

This way of looking at things changed in the 1950s. A group of men in the economics department at the University of Chicago started to believe that all human activity could be analysed using economic models, even women's economic activities. We were rational individuals not only because we competed for our next bonus or haggled at car dealerships, but also because we cleaned behind the sofa, hung up the laundry or gave birth to children, they thought. And the most famous of these economists was a young man from Pennsylvania named Gary Becker.

Together with other researchers at Chicago, Gary Becker started to include phenomena like housework, discrimination and family life in the economic models.

One might think it strange that this happened at Chicago, a school characterized by a hard, neoliberal agenda, famous for its economic fanaticism.

The department had blossomed after the war and had become known as a stronghold for economic critics of state involvement in the market. Here, from the banks of Lake Michigan, deregulation and decreased taxation were shouted about more loudly than anywhere else. Milton Friedman, who later inspired right-wing politicians like Margaret Thatcher in an almost religious way, came here in 1946; his friend George Stigler followed in 1958.

So, why did economists, specifically those at Chicago, start to care about women?

In 1979 the French philosopher Michel Foucault held a series of lectures at Collège de France in Paris. It was the same year that Thatcher would become the prime minster of Great Britain and the new right's ideas had started to gain legitimacy. Foucault was very worried. He spoke of Gary Becker and the Chicago School's idea that every part of society

31

could be analysed with the help of economic logic. All people were like economic man, Becker asserted, and so economic logic was all we needed to understand the world. Whichever aspect we wanted to study. Everything was economics. And the discipline of economics should therefore be expanded into a theory about the whole world.

This Gary Becker was interesting as a phenomenon, Foucault thought, but his ideas were far too extreme. Main-stream economics would never go this far down the path of economic imperialism, Gary Becker's thinking was just too much. Not even the burgeoning neoliberal right could ever accept these kind of theories. They were simply too absurd. Thirteen years later, in 1992, Gary Becker was awarded the Nobel Memorial Prize in Economic Sciences.

At that time, Michel Foucault had been dead for seven years, and Gary Becker's definition of economics – that it was a logic that can be applied to the whole world – had become universal. Economic man had become dominant to such an extent that economists no longer cared if an activity created tangible goods with a price tag. In the world of economic man, everything had a price tag – the only thing that differed was the currency. And suddenly even traditionally feminine tasks could be analysed economically.

The Chicago economists were the first to take women seriously as part of the economy. The problem was their method. As economist Barbara Bergmann writes: to say that they 'are not feminist in their orientation would be as much of an understatement as to say that Bengal tigers are not vegetarians'.

The Chicago economists examined the world that society had assigned to women. Armed with their economic models, they went out to uncover what they already knew. Because they already had the answer: economic man. A dream of order where everything could be boiled down to the same broth. Objective, clean and completely clear. A system of inevitabilities.

Indeed, women for thousands of years had been systematically excluded from the parts of society that held economic and political power, but this just must have been a careless mistake. A woman can of course be an economic person, just like a man. If he was independent, isolated and competitive, she could be too. She must be like that, how else would she be?

The Chicago economists started to ask completely new questions using the same economic logic. Why do people get married? they wondered. To maximize their own utility. Why do people bring children into the world? To maximize their own utility. Why do people get divorced? To maximize their own utility. The economists wrote their formulas and wrote out their equations. Look, look, it works! Even with women.

If women earned less, it must be because they deserved to be paid less, they reasoned. The world was a rational place and the market was always right – if the market decided that women should earn less, then it must be what women deserved. The economist's task was simply to explain why the market, even in this case, was making a correct assessment.

Women's lower wages were a result of women being less productive, Chicago economists concluded. Women weren't lazy or less talented, but it was quite simply not rational for a woman to make the same effort at work as a man. After all, a woman would take a break in her career for a few years to give birth. There was no reason for her to seek further education or to try as hard. Therefore women invested less in their careers and therefore were paid less.

This analysis became influential. But when the theories were compared with reality, it was clear that the explanations weren't sound. Many women were as highly educated as some men and still earned less – no matter how hard they worked. There seemed to be something called 'discrimination', and how could the Chicago economists explain that?

Gary Becker's theory about racial discrimination is their best-known attempt. Becker asserted that racial discrimination happened because certain people quite simply preferred to not mix with black people. If all people were rational and discrimination occurred, then even discrimination must be rational.

A customer who happens to be a racist might prefer not to go to a restaurant that serves black people, in the same way that he might prefer to drink his coffee with four splashes of milk. This also implies that black shop assistants might scare off certain customers, reasoned Becker. And to compensate, employers pay black people less. White workers who are racists might also demand compensation because they are forced to work with black people, and racist customers might demand lower prices: if you want to entice racist customers in spite of having black employees, you have to compensate them for having black hands pack your goods in the storeroom. And all of this combined decreases black people's wages.

Gary Becker thought that discrimination was unpleasant. But he was convinced that the market could solve even this. All we needed to do was to do nothing.

Store A, which only has white customers, would eventually be driven out of business by Store B, which would become more profitable precisely because it employed black people and had a lower overhead. Moreover, companies would realize that it was cheaper to split the work force. Blacks and whites could work in different stores within the same company – then the employer wouldn't have to compensate white racists with higher wages. In other words: everything will be fair, and everyone will earn less.

The problem was that it didn't turn out as the economists had expected. Discrimination didn't stop – of black people or of women. With regard to gender discrimination, they had other explanations to hand. This was Gary Becker's theory about housework:

What does a married woman do when she comes home from work? She wipes down the counters, irons the laundry and does homework with the children. What does a married man do when he comes home? Reads the newspaper, watches TV and maybe plays with the children for a spell, Becker imagined.

Career women simply spend more of their free time on housework, and that's more tiring than being off-duty. Here, according to Becker, lay the explanation as to why it is rational to pay women less. All that story-reading and counter-wiping made them much more tired than men. So, they couldn't make as much of an effort at the office.

At the same time, economists asserted the opposite – that the reason women did more housework was because they earned less. Because women earned less money, the family lost less on the woman being at home.

In other words, women's lower wages were because they did more housework, but the fact that women did more housework meant, in turn, that they had lower wages.

The Chicago School calculated in circles.

Other theories about women and housework were based on the idea that women were quite simply made for it. If it was true that more women did the dishes, wiped children's noses and made lists of the things that needed to be bought, then it must be because this was the most efficient division of labour. Economists modelled families as single units with a single will, a kind of small business that acted independently out of a shared utility function.

The man picked up his briefcase and the woman picked up the oven glove because the woman was better at housework. If the man had picked up the oven glove, it would be less efficient and the family as a whole would lose out. How can economists know this? Well, if the family didn't benefit from women tending to the home, then men would be the ones tending to the home. And they weren't.

They didn't formulate any actual arguments for why women were more efficient domestically. If they wrote anything at all, they stated briefly that it had to do with biology.

When legitimating the patriarchy, one is almost always referred back to the body. To be human is to subordinate the body to the intellect, and woman was not thought capable of doing this, and therefore she shouldn't have human rights either, society reasoned. Woman became 'body' so man could be 'soul'. She was bound more and more tightly to a corporeal reality so he could be freed from it.

In other words, it was easy for the Chicago economists to refer to biology. For hundreds of years the assertion that something is natural has meant that it could not and should not be changed. We've been taught to think about the relationship between what's natural and what's possible in this way. We assume that biological facts carry political conclusions, rules as impossible to rebel against as nature itself. The fact that there are biological differences between men and women is seen to justify a certain kind of politics, and it is thought that the only way to reject this kind of politics is to deny that there are biological differences. But it isn't a question of biological differences. The question is what conclusions do we draw from them? That the woman bears the child means that the woman bears the child. Not that she should stay home and nurse it until it starts college.

That the woman's cocktail of hormones contains more oestrogen means that the woman's cocktail of hormones contains more oestrogen. Not that she shouldn't teach mathematics.

That only the woman has a body part with the sole purpose of giving her pleasure means that only the woman has a body part with the sole purpose of giving her pleasure. Not that she doesn't belong on a board of directors.

Sigmund Freud did indeed assert that women were inherently better at cleaning. The father of psychoanalysis thought it was because of the vagina's inherent filth. Women scrubbed, wiped and dusted to compensate for a feeling in their own bodies. But now, Freud didn't know much about vaginas, did he?

A woman's sexual organ is an elegant self-regulated system – much cleaner than, for example, our mouths. Countless lactobacilli (the kind you also find in yoghurt) work around the clock to keep things tidy.

When the vagina is healthy, it's a little more acidic than black coffee (pH-5) but less acidic than a lemon (pH-2). Freud didn't know what he was talking about.

There is nothing in a woman's biology that makes her better suited to unpaid housework. Or to wearing herself out in a vastly underpaid job in the public sector. If you want to legitimate the global relationship between economic power and having a penis, you'll have to look elsewhere. The Chicago economists never got that far. And even working within their framework, one starts to wonder. Is it really rational to have total specialization within a household? Is it actually 'valuable' to have one adult devote themselves to housework and the other to a career? Even if the world is totally rational, how reasonable is it for a family to decide that the one adult should spend all their time on unpaid housework and the other all their time on paid work outside the home? Irrespective of who does what, is this division of labour really efficient?

Yes, perhaps if you have fourteen children, no dishwasher and cloth nappies that have to be boiled in a large tub in the garden. When housework takes that kind of time and effort, having one person devote themselves to it is likely to be more efficient. The tasks are difficult and complex, and because you spend all your waking hours on them you'll get better at doing them. That one person's specialization makes the family as a whole more productive. But in a modern society and in a family with fewer children – it can't be that great a gain. Pushing a button on the dishwasher or changing the bag in the vacuum cleaner doesn't happen much more quickly if you've been doing it full-time for a decade. But the Chicago economists weren't such progressive thinkers.

Furthermore, their reasoning assumes that the experiences one gains doing housework aren't useful on the open market. The person who takes responsibility for domestic life loses work experience, so it's only natural that he or she will earn a lower wage, they reasoned. That is, what you learn from unpaid work in the home only applies to the home.

But who says that you don't become a better boss by getting a household to run smoothly? Who says that one, for example, can't become a sharper analyst by taking care of children? As a parent, you're an economist, diplomat, handyman, politician, cook and nurse.

Play, patience, compromise. The big questions: Mum, why is the sky blue? Dad, why does the kangaroo carry its baby on its stomach? Mum, how long is forever?

When one, like the Chicago economists, supposes that a household has a shared utility function, all the conflicts within a family become invisible. In reality, income earned outside the home can have an impact on power relationships within a family and can in turn influence the choices a family makes. Mum has less say because Dad pays the bills.

That competition and buying power are important everywhere except within a family is – like so much else that's part of what we call economics – an absurd hypothesis.

However economists calculated it, in principle they always concluded that woman's subordination was rational. Her lower economic position around the world must be a function of free will, what else could it be the result of?

The picture of the individual in the story of economics is bodiless and is therefore said to be unsexed. At the same time, economic man possesses every quality that our culture traditionally attributes to masculinity. He is rational, distant, objective, competitive, alone, independent, selfish, driven by common sense and in the process of conquering the world.

He knows what he wants, and he strikes out to get it.

Everything that he isn't – feeling, body, dependence, kinship, self-sacrifice, tenderness, nature, unpredictability, passivity, connection – is what has traditionally been associated with women.

But that's just a coincidence, say economists.

When the Chicago economists discovered that women exist, they added them to the model as if they were just like him. But that proved more difficult than Gary Becker anticipated. Since Adam Smith's time, the theory about economic man has hinged on someone else standing for care, thoughtfulness and dependency. Economic man can stand for reason and freedom precisely because someone else stands for the opposite. The world can be said to be driven by self-interest because there's another world that is driven by something else. And these two worlds must be kept apart. The masculine by itself. The feminine by itself.

If you want to be part of the story of economics you have to be like economic man. You have to accept his version of masculinity. At the same time, what we call economics is always built on another story. Everything that is excluded so the economic man can be who he is.

So he can be able to say that there isn't anything else.

Somebody has to be emotion, so he can be reason. Somebody has to be body, so he doesn't have to be. Somebody has to be dependent, so he can be independent. Somebody has to be tender, so he can conquer the world. Somebody has to be self-sacrificing, so he can be selfish.

Somebody has to prepare that steak so Adam Smith can say their labour doesn't matter.

CHAPTER FOUR

*In which we see that our pact with economic man
isn't turning out as we had expected*

'Economics is about money and why it is good,' said Woody
Allen, and it's necessary to add that it's not quite that simple.

The British economist John Maynard Keynes once
calculated that each pound that the sailor Francis Drake had
plundered from Spain in 1580 and brought home to Queen
Elizabeth had grown to be worth 100,000 pounds 350 years
later. The total sum was as large as the British Empire's total
wealth outside Europe at the height of its powers.

Keynes wrote this in 1930. Wall Street had crashed the
year before and the world was on its way into the Great
Depression. Eleven thousand American banks would fail,
unemployment would come close to 25% and about half of all
American children would grow up without enough food. The
repercussions would be global. World trade would come to a
standstill, fascism would march forward and darkness would
fall over Europe. Keynes's own Great Britain had been in a
depression since the middle of the 1920s. The times were far
from rosy. But John Maynard Keynes was an optimist.

He thought that a similar process to the investments that

had made Francis Drake's stolen pounds grow could solve the economic problems of the twentieth century. If only we invested our resources correctly, they'd multiply. Interest on interest, and a century later no one would have to go hungry again.

The world's economic problems could be managed. We could and should develop beyond them. Then one day they wouldn't be anything but memories from a more evil and meagre time. The inferior housing, the lack of food, the failings in the healthcare system. Poverty. Hopelessness. Hunger. Children who starve. And adults with empty eyes.

The solution was called economic growth. If only we got the economy to grow, people, at least in Europe and the USA, could stop worrying around 2030. According to Keynes's calculations, we would be so well off that we could eventually stop working. Instead, we could devote ourselves to art, poetry, spiritual values, philosophy, taking pleasure in life, and admiring the 'lilies of the field'. This was how Keynes described it.

Growth was the medium – the lilies of the field, the goal.

It appeared to John Maynard Keynes, as he sat writing in London's Bloomsbury in 1930, that people had to organize their lives around the market. It was simply the only way to solve the world's material problems, unfortunately. Many of the things that the market brought with it Keynes found unpleasant, to say the least.

Jealousy, greed and competition. In the past 200 years, we have had to raise these values up as if they were the height of morality, said the British economist. Without egotistical bees there won't be any honey. We had no other choice. We have to pretend that just is unjust and unjust is just, wrote Keynes, because unjust is useful and just isn't. Greed works.

Unfortunately.

Like Adam Smith, Keynes thought that love was scarce. Self-interest was the locomotive that could get the economic train rolling. And get rolling it must. Just look at all the poverty. Coming to terms with material needs had to be the priority. Lilies, spirituality and all the rest could wait. Even Mahatma Gandhi said, 'There are people in the world so hungry, that God cannot appear to them except in the form of bread.'

Economic man and the ideals he stood for would make us rich. Then we could throw him overboard. Economics was the medium, lilies of the field were the goal. Let us enjoy them later. Right now, there isn't time. For Keynes, economic man was a useful idiot – someone who we eventually could afford to rid ourselves of. Thank you and farewell.

When we solved our economic problems we could allow ourselves to see economic man for who he was. 'One of those semi-criminal, semi-pathological propensities which one hands over with a shudder to the specialists in mental disease,' as Keynes himself said.

He looked forward to the day when people could devote themselves to the true art of living. When our economic problems were solved, this stuff about the economy could be put to one side. It should be a matter for a small group of specialists, 'like dentistry'.

'If economists could manage to get themselves thought of as humble, competent people on a level with dentists, that would be splendid!' Keynes famously wrote.

He could hardly have hoped more in vain.

*

In a way, John Maynard Keynes was right. We have become rich. The world's economic development has exceeded all expectations. And that the economy would develop at all was far from apparent at the gloomy start of the 1930s. John Maynard Keynes was indeed an optimist, he believed in the power of growth. But even he could never have imagined the phenomenon that is modern China, a country that has had a 9-per-cent growth rate for three decades and a middle class that has grown from 174 million to 806 million people in fifteen years.

China is exceptional. But even growth in the West has exceeded Keynes's hopes. Add to this the incredible advancements in everything from medicine to biochemistry, computer technology, telecommunications and transport. If this is to the credit of economic man, then he certainly has his good points.

As for the state of being that Keynes imagined would come next – calm, happiness, lilies, economists like nice, competent dentists – few things seem further off.

Our societies are more obsessed with economics than ever. The 'economic' way of thinking, that Keynes imagined would be put to one side to leave room for other things, has ingrained itself more deeply in the culture.

John Maynard Keynes thought that we could make a pact with economic ideals: they would help us create prosperity, and then they'd let us live our lives.

Better lives than what would otherwise have been possible.

And economic man has indeed created prosperity. But then economic man hasn't taken a step back.

He has taken over.

And economics hasn't moved into the background so that

we can devote ourselves to art, spiritual matters and enjoying life as Keynes imagined. Quite the opposite. Economics has instead been applied to everything – including art, spiritual matters and enjoying life.

Booksellers and kiosks stock stacks of books like *Freakonomics*, *Discover Your Inner Economist*, or why not: *Find a Husband After 35 Using What I Learned at Harvard Business School*. Bestselling books that instruct you on how to apply the principles of the market to everything from your love life to your next visit to the GP. *Freakonomics* has sold more than four million copies around the world. Its starting point is that the market's logic can explain everything about people, how we think and how we act. With the help of economics you can calculate the whole shebang: from the benefits of vanilla ice cream to the value of a human life.

If you like spending time with your grandmother and eating chocolate pudding, then there will always be some amount of chocolate pudding that could compensate you for never seeing your grandmother again, say the standard economic models. And it's claimed that they can tell us most things about life.

This trend isn't just found in popular science books. At universities, economists analyse ever greater parts of existence as if it were a market. From suicide (the value of a life can be calculated like the value of a company, and now it's time to shut the doors) to faked orgasms (he doesn't have to study how her eyes roll back, her mouth opens, her neck reddens and her back arches – he can calculate whether she really means it).

The question is what Keynes would think about an American economist like David Galenson. Galenson has developed a statistical method to calculate which works of art are meaningful. If you ask him what the most renowned work of the last century is, he'll say *'Les Demoiselles d'Avignon'*. He has calculated it.

Things put into numbers immediately become certainties.

Five naked female prostitutes on Carrer d'Avinyó in Barcelona. Threatening, square, disconnected bodies, two with faces like African masks. The large oil painting that Picasso completed in 1907 is, according to Galenson, the most important artwork of the twentieth century, because it appears most often as an illustration in books. That's the measure he uses. The same type of economic analysis that explains the price of leeks or green fuel is supposed to be able to explain our experience of art.

Economics is no longer the medium that will set us free from the material so that we can then take pleasure in art, as Keynes had thought. Economics is the logic through which we should view art.

And everything else.

It's one thing to discuss what makes a work of art economically valuable: why one work is worth 12 million and another 100 million. It's a completely different thing to say, as did Charles Gray, co-author of *The Economics of Art and Culture*: 'We all want to believe that there is something special about the arts, but I don't buy that there is a difference between artistic and economic value.'

Then one is asserting that an econometric analysis of value can be applied to everything. That the econometric analysis of value is the only one that exists. Economics isn't the science that will make it possible for us to devote ourselves to more important things. On the contrary, economic logic is the only thing that is real at all.

Keynes wanted mankind to dissolve its pact with economic man eventually. Greed is good; that was just something we said.

In spite of material growth, 'the economic problem' is far from being solved. If we play the game and divide the world's annual growth into equal parts, one for each of earth's six and a half billion inhabitants, then we land at about 11,000 dollars per person and no one has to go hungry again. If we stop playing the game and take a look around, things look very different.

Half of the world's population lives on less than two dollars a day. The majority of these people are women. Poverty has become a women's issue, and for millions of women the pursuit of a better life means a life far away, often far away from their own children – either loving someone else's children for pay or as a cleaner, waitress, factory worker, agricultural worker, sex worker or anything on the dark side of the global economy.

Incredibly rich countries border incredibly poor countries, incredibly rich people live just blocks from the incredibly poor, both in rich and poor countries. The global economy has brought together the western woman and her less privileged sisters from the south and east. Today, they often live under the same roof – but not in the same world. They meet as employer and employee. Master and servant.

Every year approximately half a million women die in childbirth. Most of them would have survived if they had had access to medical care. Although there isn't an international organization out there that doesn't pen beautiful press releases about how women are the key to development in poor countries, the world continues to systematically fail to invest in education and healthcare for women. In the world's richest country, the United States of America, the risk that a woman will die in childbirth is higher than in forty other countries.

Men's lives are valuable. Women's lives are valuable in relation to men's. Healthcare and food are given to men before they are given to women. This results in high casualty rates among women in parts of North Africa, China and South Asia. A boy brings economic value to a family, and access to modern technology has made it possible to see what sex the foetus is while still in the womb. Abortions of girls because they are girls occur in South Asia, China and South Korea, and also in Singapore and Taiwan.

In China there are 107 men per 100 women. In India 108. The economist Amartya Sen calculated that if women had received equal care and nourishment, there would be 100 million more women on earth.

These 100 million 'missing women' are the most extreme consequence of a system where 70% of the world's poor are women. Where 1% of the USA's population alone earns a quarter of the cumulative income. Where rich families in Hong Kong, Palm Springs and Budapest allow their homes to be cleaned and their children cared for by housekeepers and nannies who themselves live in slums.

Today's world has economic problems of a kind that Keynes could never have imagined. The poor die of malnutrition in the South but of obesity in the West. A wealthy American state like California spends more money on prisons than on universities.

Parents work so hard to buy things for their families that they don't have time to see them. Most people worry that the money won't be enough – even in the comfortable middle classes.

At the same time, a world of endless consumption and total social segregation has been fantasized forth for a small global elite. It's their existence that is held up as an ideal. Not Keynes's lilies. The famous economist assumed we'd work less and consume less when we became richer.

Imagine how wrong one can be.

On 12 December 1991, long before he became Deputy Secretary of the Treasury under Bill Clinton, President of Harvard University or Director of the White House United States National Economic Council for Barack Obama, Lawrence Summers signed an internal memo. At this time, Summers was Chief Economist at the World Bank and the paper was sent on to four other people.

'Just between you and me,' wrote Summers, 'shouldn't the World Bank be encouraging MORE migration of the dirty industries to the LDCs [Least Developed Countries]?' He continued: 'I've always thought that under-populated countries in Africa are vastly UNDER-polluted ... I think the economic logic behind dumping a load of toxic waste in the lowest wage country is impeccable and we should face up to that.'

The memo wasn't written by Summers himself, it was later established. A young economist who worked for him had written it. Lawrence Summers had read the text and put his name on the memo to give it weight. Summers also defended the memo as if it were his own. The economic logic was of course 'impeccable'. Yet he maintained that the argument had been taken out of context. The memo was written to provoke. And it certainly did. The memo was leaked to the media, and environmentalists hit the roof. How could a UN organization like the World Bank reason in this way? Should we dump toxic waste on poor people?

The *Economist* magazine, which published the Summers text, approached the matter with greater calm, the tone was of course 'crass, even for an internal memo', they thought, but the economic logic was as Summers said, 'impeccable'.

For a person who hasn't taken a foundation course in economics this might be hard to follow. But one must first understand that 'economic logic' isn't just a kind of logic, but a grand story about the meaning of human existence.

Because people's core motivation is economic, economists are the ones who understand people. They can tell us how we should organize the world so that it can best benefit our innermost nature. Which is of course to profit from things.

Find the lowest price – at all costs.

Summers' reasoning is that if we move dirty industries from Frankfurt to Mombasa both Frankfurt and Mombasa will benefit. Frankfurt will have a healthier environment and Mombasa will have more employment opportunities. Let them eat pollution.

It may sound crass, and that's the point: others may have more beautiful stories. But it's the economist's story that is true. Economic man is who we are, whether we want it or not, say the standard models of economics.

The environmentally damaging waste will of course create problems for the residents of Mombasa. Just like it did for the residents of Frankfurt. But '[t]he demand for a clean environment for aesthetic and health reasons is likely to have very high income elasticity', as it says in the Summers memo. He calculated that an increased chance of, say, prostate cancer is worse for people in a country where they live long enough to develop prostate cancer. In countries where the mortality rates for children under five years of age are at 20%, one is likely to have more pressing things to worry about.

The West exporting an increased risk of prostate cancer with its waste will be the least of Mombasa's residents' problems. They'll take the offer. They need the money, and they need the employment opportunities. It must be rational. Otherwise they wouldn't agree. Because everything people do is rational.

Imagine, the economists say, that Kenya isn't a country, but an individual. We can just as well imagine that a country is an individual. Countries act exactly like rational individuals. Imagine, then, that Germany is also a rational individual, and we'll call Kenya 'Mr K' and Germany 'Mr G'.

Mr K is poor and hungry. Mr G is rich and sated. But Mr G also has a large bucket of radioactive waste. So, Mr G offers Mr K 200 euros to take care of his waste for him.

Two hundred euros isn't very much money for Mr G. But 200 euros is an incredible amount for Mr K. And because Mr K doesn't mind about it being radioactive (he's busy being hungry), he accepts the offer. Everyone gets richer. Everyone is happy. Everyone wins.

This reasoning is built on the idea that we are all calculating, rational individuals with self-evident, stable preferences.

The model doesn't take into consideration what would happen if Mr G, for example, had to live with his waste at home in his flat in Frankfurt. Maybe then Mr G would have found a long-term technical solution. In this case, he can only sell the problem to Mr K. And Mr K is too poorly educated to develop a long-term solution. The world will therefore never find one. And in the long run society will lose out. How rational is that?

These possibilities are part of a scenario that the model doesn't take into account. It doesn't matter how hungry Mr K is. He is still a rational, calculating individual with total control over what he does. He agrees to act as Mr G's dump because it is rational to do so. The impeccable economic logic only sees two individuals on a desert island, each with a need. There is no context, no future, no connection.

'Your reasoning is perfectly logical but completely insane,' José Lutzenberger, then Brazil's Secretary of the Environment, wrote to Lawrence Summers.

Impeccable economic logic is one thing. The region around the town of Guiyu in China is another.

Every year one million tonnes of electronic waste are sent to Guiyi, in China's Guangdong province. One hundred and fifty thousand people work to sort it and break it down. Most of them are part of small family businesses, and many are women.

Computers, screens, printers, DVD players, photocopying machines, car batteries, microwave ovens, speakers, telephone chargers and telephones. With small tools and with bare hands they pick everything apart. Circuit boards are boiled away to retrieve the chip. Wires are burned to release the metals.

And to extract gold from microchips, you need a corrosive, poisonous bath of acid. The earth around the city is full of lead, chrome, tin and other heavy metals. The groundwater is poisoned. The river is black. The lead levels in children's blood are 88% higher than in neighbouring areas.

Chinese law forbids the importing of electronic waste. Beijing has even signed the Basel Convention against electronic waste being transported to poorer countries, but so far this has been ineffective. Ninety per cent of all American electronic waste is exported to either China or Nigeria.

The economic logic may be impeccable. In Guiyu the price of water is ten times higher than in the neighbouring municipality of Chendian. Because now Chendian is where they must get their water. Their own water is poisoned.

Eighty years after Keynes there are few who, like him, would define the purpose of economics as ridding the world of poverty. Economic science no longer sees itself this way.

When it comes time to choose sides, between rich and poor, powerful and powerless, workers and businesses, men and women, economists in recent decades have landed on the same side. What is good for the rich and powerful is almost always 'good for the economy'. Meanwhile, economic science has become increasingly abstract: fictional households, fictional businesses and fictional markets. Everything based on economic man.

Economists have become more and more interested in trying to apply their models to everything from racism to orgasms and less and less interested in studying how real markets work.

At the same time the problems that Keynes worried about are far from solved. In many cases, they have also been made invisible.

When we are all rational individuals, questions like race, class and sex become irrelevant. Why, we are all free. Like the woman in the Congo. She who agrees to militia men having sex with her in exchange for three tins of food. Or the woman in Chile. She who works as a fruit picker even though the exposure to pesticides will lead to nerve damage in the child she will give birth to two years later. Or the woman in Morocco. She who takes a job in a factory and then has to force her oldest daughter to quit school so she can care for her siblings. They always have a complete overview of the consequences of their actions. They always make the best possible decisions.

Freedom's just another word, indeed it's just another word.

Economists are convinced that they are modelling the deepest causes of human behaviour. Their critics are only scratching the surface – if you torture the data enough, eventually it will reveal the truth: everything is economic man.

One logic. One world. One way of being. What lilies?

CHAPTER FIVE

In which we add women and stir

'I have the biggest cock in the building,' Judith Regan, one of the USA's most feared businesswomen, used to shout from her desk at the publishing house she ran.

We're starting to become the men we used to want to marry, the women's movement triumphantly exclaimed in the seventies.

Women went from wanting to have a man to wanting what men had. In spite of the progress that this implied, the project was still about the same thing: men.

'We did it!' the *Economist* magazine exclaimed on the cover of its new year's issue in 2010. Women had overtaken men and now made up the majority of all university graduates in OECD countries. In most wealthy countries, more women than ever are entering the workplace. They are running companies that had previously treated them like second-class citizens.

But the very notion of a full-time career is still built around full-time domestic help. Today, women are supposed to work full-time, but full-time help is only available to those who can afford it. Who cleans the cleaner's house? Who takes care of the nanny's daughter? These aren't just rhetorical questions, they are issues where the answer can only be found by following a complicated network of care wrapped around the global economy.

Today over half of the world's migrants are women. In certain countries this number reaches between 80 and 90%. Their lives are made up of long workdays and low wages. Housework is difficult. Isolated and unregulated. She often lives where she works – in someone else's home. She is a part of the family – but also not.

The quality of her work is decided to a large degree by the relationships she has been able to form. If she bonds with the family, she'll be a better nanny. The children will see her more often than Mum, and definitely more than Dad. In some cases, they'll love her. But if she bonds with the family it will be more difficult when it's time to renegotiate her salary and terms of employment. It will be almost impossible to separate the roles. Is she working out of self-interest, out of love – or both?

The employer often thinks that they can take advantage of this predicament.

If the nanny does a poor job, she'll have failed, but if she does too good a job she'll also have failed. If the children grow more attached to her than to Mum and Dad, Mum and Dad won't be pleased. The nanny's career will be short-lived. It's a difficult balancing act.

The working hours of domestic labourers around the world are among the longest, most precarious and most un-predictable of any jobs on the labour market. Many women in this sector aren't allowed to leave the house without permission, according to a study conducted by Human Rights Watch. Verbal, physical and sexual harassment is common, but seldom reported. Moreover, such a worker is often in the country illegally and afraid of being deported. She worries almost all the time. Mostly about her children on the other side of the planet.

This is one side of the equation.

The other is that a Filipina housekeeper in Hong Kong earns as much money as a male doctor in the rural Philippines. And that foreign nannies working in Italy have a salary that is between seven and fifteen times higher than what they could earn in their home countries. Are they victims? If so, compared with whom?

In this way, she provides for herself and her family. It gives her power. Over her father and her ex-husband. Power and freedom. The money that female migrants send home contributes more to the economy of many countries than aid and foreign investments combined. In the Philippines it accounts for 10% of GDP.

On the other hand, if a cleaner's hourly wage doesn't continue to be markedly less than the hourly wage of the person who would otherwise be doing the cleaning (the woman in the western family), then it won't be economical to hire domestic help. The situation, in other words, implies a continued inequality between women.

The woman has entered the paying job market, and she has been able to buy herself free from doing large portions of the housework. She had to. If you're going to have a career you check your family life at the door when you arrive at the office.

Time to perform, time to be selfish. Time to lean in. But to what?

The job market is still largely defined by the idea that humans are bodiless, sexless, profit-seeking individuals without family or context. The woman can choose between being one of these, or being their opposite: the invisible and self-sacrificing one who is needed to balance the equation.

And often her situation makes this decision for her.

The feminist economist Marilyn Waring looked at the unpaid labour carried out by a young woman in the Lowveld in Zimbabwe. She wakes up at 4 a.m. to carry a bucket eleven kilometres to the well and back. Three hours later, she has returned home with the water. Still barefoot. Collecting wood, washing dishes, cooking lunch, doing the dishes again and then out to get vegetables. Fetching water a second time, dinner, younger siblings needing to be tucked in and the workday is over at nine. According to the economic models, she's unproductive, not working, economically inactive.

Mincing the meat, setting the table, drying the dishes, dressing the children, driving to school. Sorting the rubbish, dusting the window ledges, sorting the dirty laundry, mangling the sheets, repairing the lawnmower, getting petrol for the car, picking up books, clearing away the Legos, answering the phone, hoovering the hall, doing homework, washing the floor, cleaning the stairs, making the beds, paying the bills, scrubbing the sink and tucking in the children.

The main argument for not including housework in GDP is usually that it doesn't matter. The amount of housework will always be the same in a society. But how can economists know this if they never include it in their statistics?

A woman in our world spends just over two-thirds of her working day on unpaid work. The equivalent statistic for men is one quarter. In developing countries with large agricultural sectors, the difference is even greater. In Nepal, women work twenty-one hours more each week than men. In India, around twelve.

In parts of Asia and Africa where men often migrate to the cities, women are left behind. They have no support from men or from the state, but still they have to manage the triple burden of a career, housework and agricultural work.

Economists sometimes joke that if a man marries his house-keeper, the GDP of the country declines. If, on the other hand, he sends his mother to an old-age home, it increases again. In addition to the joke saying a lot about the perception of gender roles among economists, it also shows how the same kind of work can be counted or not counted as part of the GDP.

When married women entered the workforce, they started to devote more time to the kind of work that is counted (working outside the home) and less time to the kind of work that isn't (domestic work). This dramatically increased the GDP in the western world. But is this increase accurate? Because no one had bothered to quantify housework, we might have overvalued the actual increase of wealth. Indeed, washing machines, microwaves and mixers have made housework less time consuming – so the difference isn't necessarily that great. But the point is that we don't know.

If you want the full picture of the economy you can't ignore what half of the population is doing half of the time.

*

Housework is neither more nor less difficult to measure than much of what we include in GDP. For example, we take great pains to measure the value of the food a farmer produces on his land but doesn't take to market. With housework, we don't make the same effort. Women's work is a natural resource that we don't think we need to account for. Because we assume it will always be there. It's considered an invisible, indelible infrastructure.

Canada's national statistical agency tried to measure the value of unpaid work. Between 30.6 and 41.4% of the GDP, they concluded. The first number is calculated on the basis of how much it would cost to replace unpaid work with paid. The other is based on how much a person would earn if they were earning a wage while they were doing housework.

Whatever the method – the sum is enormous.

To blossom economically, a society must have people, knowledge and trust. And these resources are nurtured largely with unpaid domestic work. Happy, healthy children are the foundation of all forms of positive development – even economic. Economic man, on the other hand, has neither a childhood nor a context. He grows out of the ground like a mushroom. And when all people are assumed to be like him, a large part of the economy becomes impossible to see.

In practice, it's one way to exclude women.

To uphold the idea that economic man is universal, woman must be stuffed into the model as if she were just like him. Here you are, here are equal rights and equal freedom to compete in the marketplace. Go forth and conquer!

That's why a woman has to prove her worth in a job market that is essentially still shaped by the needs of men. Advance herself in a framework created by men, for men – from a reality that excludes women. And this creates problems.

You can't just add women and stir.

In 1957 Betty Friedan, then a thirty-six-year-old mother of two, sent out a questionnaire to her former classmates. It had been fifteen years since they had graduated from Smith College and they were due to meet again at a class reunion. Most of the alumni from this elite women's school, like Friedan, were completely taken up with tending to their homes and children. But Friedan also worked as a freelance writer. She had been fired from her job as a journalist when she became pregnant, and before their class reunion, she wanted to find out how her former classmates viewed their lives and thought she might write an article about it.

Betty Friedan included a few questions of a more psychological nature and sent out the questionnaire. The answers that were returned to her were shocking. Most of these women who had it all on paper were actually deeply unhappy. And this was the most forbidden of feelings.

The anxiety, the sexual frustration, the hopelessness and depression – the real feelings of real housewives stood in stark contrast to the images of happy women in happy suburbs churned out by the media. This was post-war America: the Space Race, record growth and smiling children on the drive. Friedan didn't know what she should call her discovery. There was no language available to discuss it, and she started to call it 'the problem that has no name'.

Dissatisfied, confused, drugged with sedatives, led astray by psychoanalysis and ignored by society, these were the real housewives. Friedan wrote an article. No periodical would publish it, and in the end she had no other choice but to develop the material into a book.

In 1963 *The Feminine Mystique* was published in the USA. Betty Friedan wrote of how upper-middle-class women cried in their pillows, confined in perfect suburban homes. How the vision of a life focused on catching a man, keeping a man, having children and blowing off your own needs was gnawing away at them slowly from the inside. How it was an ideal that had to be swallowed together with miracle pills so it could be choked down. How women were tricked into the idea that they were childish, delicate things made for domestic life, breeding and consumerism. If they wanted something else, then there was something wrong with them: take a pill, have an affair, buy a washing machine. The book sold more than two million copies and 'pulled the trigger on history', as the American author Alvin Toffler put it.

The limits of what women could achieve, be, think, say and get turned on by were demolished over the course of a single generation. It happened so quickly that the revolution seemed to be over before the opposing factions had time to take shape. Today, we watch Peggy, Joan and Betty in the American TV drama *Mad Men* with fascination. An advertising agency in New York at the start of the 1960s where women are ignored, objectified and made invisible in an apparently insurmountable world of self-righteous, chain-smoking white men who mirror themselves in each other and in their ever-full glasses of whiskey. Did the job market really look like this only fifty-some years ago?

But in spite of the incredible progress of the women's movement, we don't seem to have succeeded in raising daughters with high self-esteem. Girls perform better in schools today than boys – but feel much worse. Depression has become a woman's illness. Not adequate, not enough energy, not strong enough. A constant drizzle of unreasonable fears. It's not just nurses and care workers whose bodies and souls can't cope. Even women in the private sector with high salaries are breaking down at a higher rate than their male counterparts and going on long-term sick leave. Even in the fêted Scandinavian welfare states. Even though the opportunities to combine family and career are thought to be better there than anywhere else.

We talk about 'work–life balance' as a concept built on the idea of a private sphere sharply divided from a public sphere. You can travel between them, but can you change them?

Women are still fighting to gain equal access to the world of economic man. A woman must work harder to show her commitment in the office, in order to fight the assumption that her place is really in the home. At the same time she is judged on her ability to keep the home and family in order in a way that men are not. The resulting work–life conflict is portrayed as a women's issue. It's her responsibility to resolve it. Be more assertive at work, reduce your work hours, find the right partner, make better to-do lists, simplify your life, declutter your handbag, do more yoga, and keep your eye on the clock!

She is encouraged to see her body not as part of what it means to be human but as a ticking fertility bomb set to explode at the same time she's going to be up for a promotion.

Then she will be exposed for what she is: a woman.

In motherhood everything collides. The public and private

sphere that needs to be kept separate suddenly merge. She cannot leave her pregnant belly at home with the rest of her private self. She must bring something of the home into the world of paid work and back again. Herself. More of what she is.

Which neither she nor the world of paid work can handle.

Economic man doesn't have leaking breasts or hormones. He doesn't have a body.

No baby has ever vomited on him.

And no baby ever will.

Studies show that since the 1970s women in the West have felt that they have become less happy. It doesn't matter which class she comes from, whether she's married or single, how much money she earns, which country she lives in, or whether she has children. The typical woman in the West (with the exception of African American women in the United States) is less satisfied with life. Men, on the other hand, have grown happier. Maybe it's the 'equality'. Or maybe we're measuring happiness the wrong way. Maybe these kinds of things can't be measured. The studies are disputed. Across Europe both men and women report increases in happiness over the last forty years, but men have been getting happier faster. In Britain you find little difference between men's and women's happiness. The exception here is divorced fathers, who are not happy.

What women all over the developed world report, how-ever, is being more stressed and feeling more short of time than men. It's neither class- or occupation-specific. It's gender-specific. But when women admit that they feel this way, feminism is usually blamed. The fact that women are having a hard time being like economic man is taken as proof that women don't belong in the public sphere.

They say that Ginger Rogers did everything that Fred Astaire did – except that she did it backwards and in high heels. And that's what women continue to do. Woman has entered the job market but man has not entered the home to the same extent. Our ideas about the boundaries between work and family life haven't fundamentally changed. We try to cobble them together in different ways, rather than creating something new. A better way of life. Whichever way we turn, there seems to be a frightful lack of options.

We now have a generation of women who feel they are failing at 'having it all'. Many women today don't need male chain-smoking ad agency executives to look at them as if they were worthless. They look at themselves this way, even if they themselves are executives at the firm.

Gloria Steinem says feminism wasn't about women getting a bigger piece of the pie. Feminism was about baking a completely new pie.

This has proved to be easier said than done. We added women to the mix and stirred. An entire generation interpreted the slick proclamation 'You can be anything' as 'You have to be everything'. 'Having it all' became 'doing it all'.

Otherwise, you're worthless.

Half a century on from Betty Friedan's *The Feminine Mystique*, we have encountered a new 'problem that has no name'. The feminist Naomi Wolf writes that we have failed at giving our daughters a definition of success that simply lets them be.

Do more! Do it better! Beat out the competition! Economic

man became the ideal she was forced to live up to. Women's liberation as it was defined in the West became a set of tasks to perform, a checklist of aspirations to 'lean in' to. Instead it should have meant a proliferation of all sorts of freedoms.

Including the freedom to just be.

You don't need to have the biggest cock in the building. It's fine not to have a cock at all – even if you're a woman.

CHAPTER SIX

In which Las Vegas and Wall Street merge

If you find yourself on the ground with an anti-aircraft gun charged with shooting down an aeroplane high above you, it doesn't do you much good to aim for the spot where the aeroplane is now. In the time that passes between you firing the gun and the projectile reaching the plane, the plane will have moved.

What the person operating the anti-aircraft gun must do is instead aim for the point where the plane will be in a moment. Even the pilot knows this. And that's why he has an interest in flying as unpredictably as possible.

Right. Left. Left. Right.

The person on the ground can then decide between aiming left or right. If the anti-aircraft gun fires in the same direction as the pilot chooses to turn. Bang. The pilot is dead.

If the anti-aircraft gun fires in the opposite direction to the one in which the pilot is flying, the pilot will get away.

Therefore the best way for the pilot to act is to randomly and unpredictably fly to the right or left. And the best way for the man on the ground to act is to do the same thing. As soon as the pilot identifies a pattern in the gunfire, he can react accordingly and improve his chances of not being hit. The same thing applies in the inverse: if the man with the anti-aircraft gun sees that the man in the plane tends to fly left – then he has a better chance of hitting him.

In 1944 the mathematician John von Neumann concluded that the above scenario was like a zero-sum game between two participants. It doesn't matter whether the plane or the anti-aircraft gun is operated by a person or by a machine. The pilot's actions are decided by the logic of the system. It doesn't have anything to do with him as an individual.

It doesn't matter what his relationship is like with his mother, which social class he was raised in, that in a psychological test he would be categorized as having an ESTJ personality type and that he is still ashamed that he wet the bed until he was nine years old.

The pilot will act in a way that Professor von Neumann can calculate. Guided by the logic of the situation and the rules of the game that arise when rational people meet.

Instead of studying the specifics of people's lives, we should instead immerse ourselves in what people have in common with computers, thought John von Neumann. Or rather, with the gigantic clutter of valves, cables and slider controls that at this time were still called 'mathematics machines' or 'electronic brains'.

Existence is a set of games and the actions of rational participants are decided by a larger system. You put one foot in front of the other, but it's not you who is in control of your decisions. Someone has wound you up and placed you on a ledge. Mankind, the world and the progress of history is mechanical, pre-programmed and driven by impersonal powers. A ship without a captain. Adam Smith's economic man had evolved and was charging full-speed into the Space Age.

John von Neumann and Oskar Morgenstern's book *Theory of Games and Economic Behaviour* was published in 1944, and with it game theory was born. Von Neumann used the term 'game' to describe a situation where you must make a choice knowing that others are making choices too. A 'game' is a conflict where the outcome will be determined in some prescribed way by all the choices made. You 'play', but not in the way kittens and puppies do. It's more like poker: full of bluffing and second guessing, yes, but rational. Early game theory carried with it the old dream of economics: if you could just read society's book mathematically you could understand everything. John von Neumann was convinced that one could eventually explain all of society using game theory.

Von Neumann was born in Budapest in 1903 and grew up during the city's most glittering epoch: scientists, authors, artists, musicians and tons of useful, culture-loving millionaires. 'What are you calculating?' it is said a six-year-old von Neumann once asked his mother when she was staring into space.

He was named Janos, but called Johnny. His father was a Jewish banker. He had bought his aristocratic title, never used it, but passed it on to his son. At the age of eighteen von Neumann moved to Berlin and then to Zürich to study chemistry. He eventually earned a PhD in mathematics. The Second World War drew near, and von Neumann left for Princeton University. There he started working together with the Austrian Oskar

Morgenstern, who had been in the United States when Adolf Hitler annexed his homeland, and so had decided to stay on the other side of the Atlantic. Morgernstern's grandfather was said to be Fredrik the Third, emperor of Germany.

In the spring of 1945, one year after the publication of the pair's groundbreaking book, von Neumann was recruited to join the committee tasked with choosing which Japanese cities the USA's newly developed atom bomb should be used on. Von Neumann had joined the Manhattan Project two years earlier and had worked on the development of the bomb itself. He was one of several Hungarian scientists involved. When asked about this 'statistically unlikely' concentration, he would say it was 'a coincidence of some cultural factors he could not make precise: an external pressure on the whole society of this part of Central Europe, a subconscious feeling of extreme insecurity in individuals, and the necessity of producing the unusual or facing extinction'. Now he oversaw the computations for the target committee: 'the size of the bomb burst, the amount of damage expected, and the ultimate distance at which people would be killed'.

Kyoto was the first choice. But Secretary of War Henry Stimson vetoed it. The city was too historically and culturally significant. At 08.10 local time the bomb was instead dropped from 600 metres above Hiroshima: It was called 'Little Boy'. Five-thousand-degree heat that melted houses, winds that broke bridges and crushed buildings. Thousands of burning people, their skin hanging in strips from their bodies, threw themselves screaming into the Ota River where they drowned and became unidentifiable piles of corpses. And then came the radioactive rain. Those who survived the fire died of the rain.

A death that for the next months spread in ever-widening circles, like a quickly spreading rash on your skin.

A few days later a second bomb was dropped on Nagasaki.

The Second World War ended and the Cold War began. John von Neumann's game theories were absorbed into the spirit of the time. Or perhaps it was the other way around. The story fit like a glove in the reigning political climate. Economic man put on his trench coat and disappeared among the spies in the power struggle between East and West. The life and death of the planet seemed as if it would be decided by the next move of a chess piece in a game between the USA and the Soviet Union. This was before the internet and before multi-national terror cells. The players made phone calls on red telephones and discussed whether or not they should annihilate each other. There wasn't a big leap from here to viewing other relationships like a game of chess. The future firmly bound to the next stroke of logic, both claustrophobic and freeing. Everyone is a captive of the same dilemma; opponents on either side of a chessboard where each piece is moved by inevitable dictates of reason.

They say that there is a world in which Hiroshima was inevitable. The greatest minds of the last century have identified it and expressed it mathematically.

Early game theorists calculated that the best way to defeat the Soviet Union was to obliterate the country in a single atomic attack, before the Soviet Union had a chance to obliterate America first. That the dissolution of the Soviet Union would happen on the back of something like peaceful demonstrations, satellite dishes, a Polish pope, a horrible nuclear accident, rock 'n' roll, a Czech dramatist and local politicians in Leipzig who refused to shoot at civilian crowds on a regular Monday, that didn't feature in any of the models.

The idea that war and conflicts are purely rational, calculable considerations lives on today. Even if the playing fields for the superpowers' arm-wrestling matches are no longer Berlin, Vienna, Warsaw, but instead Kabul, Tehran and Peshawar. Game theorists still assert that instead of looking at the specifics of a conflict, we must look at the factors that make war predictable, whatever the context. We should study war like one 'studies cancer', they say. Instead of trying to cure individual patients and being consumed by the specifics of their cases, we should look at how the cancer cells themselves behave.

War is rational, otherwise it wouldn't exist. And the answer to getting rational people to stop fighting is simply 'increase the cost' of war. Economic man only resorts to violence when there isn't a cheaper way out. So let's give him one.

John von Neumann died in 1957. In addition to his involvement in Hiroshima, his legacy included the development of modern computing, plus a less successful suggestion to paint the polar ice caps black so Iceland could have the same climate as Hawaii. His game theory became the foundation for modern finance. Dr Strangelove went to work on Wall Street.

Economic science, with its models and theories, had long been removed from how analysts and traders bought and sold on the financial markets. This changed in the 1950s and 1960s.

A company sells stocks to raise capital, for example, to

expand its operations, open a new shop, hire more employees or renovate. Those who buy the stocks can then trade with them on the stock market for stocks in other companies. The trade results in gains and losses, the value of the stock goes up and goes down – a value that in turn impacts the company's ability to access capital. At one level of abstraction above these transactions are, for example, products like index funds and derivatives. If stocks and the stock market are bets on companies, derivative markets and index funds are bets on bets. Money that is invested here doesn't filter down into reality, but instead continues to infinitely replicate itself.

Mathematical models can make calculations on risk in these markets more easily surveyed and simpler to handle. They are good for the economy and good for society. But mathematical models should never be superordinate to reality in the way that they have become since John von Neumann's time. This has had severe consequences – most notably it resulted in the 2008 global financial crisis. By the 1980s, the finance industry was almost entirely based on abstract mathematics.

In the same way that physicists formulated laws for matter and energy, finance tried to formulate laws for stocks and derivatives.

The problem is that economics is not a science comparable to physics. You can't formulate laws for the economy in the same way that you can for energy or matter. In physics you can conduct the same experiment time and time again and get the same result each time. If you let go, the apple will fall to the ground. It's not the same in economics. As the American physicist Murray Gell-Mann once said: 'think how hard physics would be if the electrons could think'. The market is comprised of people, and they can think, and furthermore, they can feel. The market is not a game. Not unless you turn it into one.

In light of game theory's view of the world, economists started studying dice games and roulette to try and understand the market. If the world was a game, then the financial markets could be a casino. That seemed logical.

'Wall Street is like a big gambling casino. The game is much bigger and much more interesting to me than casino gambling,' said Edward Thorp.

Thorp was a mathematics professor and blackjack player who eventually became a hedge-fund manager. In 1962 he published the book *Beat the Dealer* about how one uses mathematics to win at blackjack. Five years later came *Beat the Market* about how one uses mathematics to beat the stock market. A casino's games of chance or the value of a company. Las Vegas or Wall Street. Everything merged.

When economists started building models based on dice games and roulette they were assuming the market worked in the same way. How the dice are thrown in a casino doesn't affect how they will land in the future. Within the seemingly innocent assumption that the financial market functions like a casino lies a much larger assumption that the market doesn't have a memory. Every investment or bet is completely independent of the one before. Just as the roulette ball can land on red or black, a stock can go up or down, unaffected by what has happened in the past. The market forgets and forgives. And everything starts fresh in the morning. These principles were developed into the efficient market hypothesis (EMH). The hypothesis states that the price-setting of the financial market is always representative of the best possible appraisal of what something is worth. The market is always right. Therefore bubbles should not form, and if they do, the market will correct itself.

No one should intervene.

This rationale is grounded in several assumptions. First, that all investors and buyers are completely rational. Second, that everyone has access to the exact same information about the sale. Information that they then interpret in exactly the same way. Third, that buyers and investors make decisions independently, without influencing each other.

Because information spreads with such speed, the market is assumed to know more than any one person at any given time. It is assumed that it can take in all available information automatically and immediately. Adam Smith's all-knowing invisible hand creates order in what would otherwise have been a chaos of human desires and wishes. The market becomes a higher collective consciousness that guides and disciplines us. It can never be wrong – because it's just the sum of the endless enterprise of surveying all the information there is in every price and shift on the stock market.

Theologians have compared the efficient market hypothesis to the word of God. And it's not hard to understand why.

The market knows more than you do, it can satisfy you, and at the same time it's the one making decisions. Really, this is a well-worn fantasy. But it has never before been taken further than in the efficient market hypothesis.

Adam Smith stated that there was a 'natural price' for all commodities. All prices were constantly pulled towards this. Sugar, for a number of reasons, can be more expensive or cheaper at times, but it's always being pulled towards its natural price. The economy never stands still in this state. If it did, the whole mechanism would grind to a halt. It whirrs around an equilibrium. Constantly pulled in the different directions of conflicting interests.

Eventually, a mathematical theory was developed for this story. The market is driven by supply and demand: if there are many umbrellas (large supply) and a small demand (the sun is shining), then the price of umbrellas will go down. If there are, on the other hand, few umbrellas (small supply) and a great demand (it's pouring with rain), then the price will rise.

This view of the market is more poetic than scientific. In a statistical world, there are no problems with information. All the information that is needed will flow smoothly to the person who knows how to use it. Of course, real markets don't operate with this absence of friction. But this is first and foremost a story about the inherent perfection of a market economy. We don't want things to be like they were in the Soviet Union.

It may be a comforting story. At the same time, it's pointless to ask if a market economy would function efficiently in a statistical world where all people are perfect, rational, economic men. If all people were like economic man and the world was static, any economic system would work. If everyone has all of the information and can always determine the consequences of their actions, the economy would be so predictable that it could just as well have been centrally planned in Moscow.

However sophisticated the mathematical models are that economists create, they are incapable of saying anything about reality as long as they are based on the assumption that they don't need to have anything to do with reality. The efficient market hypothesis has been called 'the biggest mistake in the history of finance'.

The market isn't a neutral machine that prices everything correctly. The financier George Soros suggests it's the opposite. The market isn't just wrong sometimes. The market is always wrong. Those who play the market approach it with a flawed view, but their flawed view impacts how things unfold. And only when one begins to understand this can one become as rich as George Soros, at least according to George Soros himself.

In the world of game theory, there is no difference if there is or isn't a person in the aeroplane that is going to be shot down. How the plane moves between the anti-aircraft gun's projectiles is decided by the logic of the system. But the financial markets aren't rational systems. They are made up of people. Economic behaviour is driven collectively and by emotions. Not individually and rationally.

The economy isn't a machine that mechanically rolls forward on millions of independently operating parts, organized by a simple blueprint – rational systems on an endless quest for equilibrium. It's a network of relationships, and the only blueprint there is comes from within and can only be understood in relation to the whole.

In the meantime, economic man in the financial theories seems to live in a world where time is a series of isolated incidents. One moment is dead as soon as the next begins: the past, the present and the future are completely separate. In reality, investors work together: captives and creators of the logic that then turns into movement in the market. The whole is made from its parts but can't be reduced to them. And time is a complex thing: the memory of yesterday and the expectations of tomorrow create the present. Expectations determine what you remember, and your memory determines your expectations.

In spite of this, the theories about the market's natural equilibrium weren't properly interrogated until the 1990s. They were quite simply too elegant. Sexy in their simple mechanics. Fun to dress up in increasingly complex numerical vestments. From Wall Street to university campuses: people wanted to believe in this dream. And so they did.

Even on 15 September 2008.

CHAPTER SEVEN

In which the global economy goes to hell

What can the second act of Johann Wolfgang von Goethe's great drama *Faust* teach us about economics? Doctor Faust has made his pact with the Devil's emissary, Mephistopheles, and when the second act of the drama begins they find themselves in the Emperor's court.

The empire is having serious economic problems. Gold is the country's currency, and there isn't enough to cover the costs. The Emperor has been spending recklessly and total financial catastrophe is nigh.

But, Emperor, the wily Mephistopheles suggests: even if there isn't enough gold, there is probably gold that has yet to be discovered. Deep down in the ground. Gold that at some point will be found. And even if this gold doesn't exist yet and we just think it exists, it still has value. Because the Emperor owns the land, he should be able to issue securities against the value of the to-be-discovered gold.

With that, the Devil's emissary introduces paper money. The emperor goes from being in debt to being debt-free. As if by magic, he is rich and his land flourishes. But the foundation of his empire has also shifted – from real gold to insubstantial promises on paper.

The potential for prosperity is huge. But so are the risks.

Goethe wasn't just one of the greatest poets in the history of the world. He was a minister of finance in Weimar.

The history of money is a journey from the material to the immaterial. When economics was in its infancy, currency was supposed to be useful and easy to count: shells, livestock and salt were best. I bought land from you for ten cows, and they were worth something for the simple reason that you could eat them and survive the cold winters. Long into modern times, the Kyrgyz people of the Russian steppes used horses as a method of payment. Sheep were a smaller denomination and lamb pelts were loose change.

In *The Philosophy of Money*, George Simmel said that our relationship to money is like our relationship to God. Money is an absolute medium of exchange, just as God is an absolute.

Money can measure all other goods. In a world without money, if you want my kettle you can only have it if I want your spade. Why else would I want to trade my kettle? You have to have something that I want for an exchange to take place. In other words, what economists call a 'mutual agreement between parties' must arise.

If money exists, on the other hand, I don't have to want your spade in order to be prepared to part with my kettle. You can give me money instead, and by saving the money, I can save the value of what I have exchanged. In the future, I can trade it for something else.

One of the functions of money is that it stores value in this way. Trade becomes much easier, and much more frequent. Instead of being completed on the spot, the full course of a trade can be put off until some time in the future.

Around 1200 BC cowry shells from the shallow water of the Indian and Pacific Oceans began to be used as money in China. At the end of the Stone Age, copies of the shells were made in bronze and copper, and with this, the first true coins were born. Eventually they were made flat and in China they often had holes in the centre so they could be strung on long chains.

Outside China, coins were silver nuggets stamped with a god or an emperor's seal. The technology developed in what is now Turkey; it was quickly spread by the Greeks, Persians and Macedonians, and later the Romans. In contrast to China, where simple metals were used, others started producing coins in gold, silver and bronze.

The world's first banknotes were made of leather, thirty-centimetre-square pieces of white deerskin edged in bright colours. Around 800 AD, paper money started being used in China. This went on for over 500 years until the system was abandoned because of inflation. The temptation to print more money was too great. Especially when new wars needed to be bankrolled. Soon the value of the banknotes had little to do with the value of anything else, and China went back to basing its economy on silver.

The currency of most countries was based either on silver or gold until a few decades ago. In 1816 the English currency was pegged to gold. At that point, paper money had been in use for hundreds of years but its value was then directly related to the precious metal. The American Gold Standard Act was passed in 1900 and led to the establishment of the Federal Reserve System. You could take your paper money to the State and the State would give you gold at a fixed exchange rate.

In 1945 the Bretton Woods system was founded. Forty-five of the Allies of the Second World War met in the little town of Bretton Woods, New Hampshire, and became part of a system where the countries had a fixed exchange rate against the dollar. The value of a country's currency was insured, they could always exchange it for dollars, and the dollars could in turn be exchanged for gold. Gold doesn't rust. And gold lasts for ever. All of the gold that has ever been found on earth could be packed in four and a half cubic kilometres. And that which is rare also becomes valuable.

In 1971 the Bretton Woods system was abandoned. Today, banknotes are just bits of paper in your wallet. They gain value in the same way that other goods gain value.

Because we want them.

You want money because other people want money. And this shared desire means that you know that you can use your money to buy goods and services. As long as you believe that money will continue to be valuable, you will continue to work to obtain it – and so the system works.

Today the job of central banks is to assure us that we can trust the dollar, the krona, the euro and the pound. They are more concerned with their credibility, their reputation and their legitimacy than with the amount of gold in some vault. It's about image, expectations and psychology. It's when we stop believing in money that the economy will fall apart.

Money is a social construction. And as for religion, so for the financial markets – in the beginning there was faith.

Twelve hundred years ago Aristotle spoke of how the philosopher Thales once predicted that the coming year's olive crop would be of record size. Thales contacted the owners at the local olive presses and offered to buy the rights to rent all of the presses during the harvest season. No one knew how the crops would turn out, and by taking Thales's money the owners could insure themselves against losses. They got in on the deal. Months passed, and it turned out that Thales was right: the olive crop was enormous. Every grower suddenly needed access to the presses. Thales had bought the right to rent them at a set price and now could charge a premium to rent them out.

Today the kind of contract that Thales brokered would be called an 'option contract'.

Innovation in finance has always been about changing and playing with the relationship between time and money in various ways. And for centuries people were sceptical of financial instruments, precisely because they play with time. Time belongs to God and God alone. The theological doctrine of usury was about how the person who lends money against interest is 'selling time'. By giving you a loan, they give you the opportunity to buy something today that you wouldn't otherwise have been able to buy until next year. The interest you pay becomes the price of the time that passes between the opportunity to take the loan and the opportunity next year.

And to put a price on time – that was blasphemy.

Aristotle said that it was unnatural to charge interest on

borrowed money because it 'makes a gain out of money itself'. Unclean money. Illegitimate money. From the perverse union of money that fucks itself. Money that gives birth to other money was seen as a sexual perversion.

It was with John Calvin and the protestant reformation that this attitude first changed. Why couldn't one earn as much or more from the growth of companies or stores than from owning land in the countryside? The tradesman's profit came from his own diligence and should belong to him; why shouldn't it be able to grow? asked Calvin, who tried to adapt Christianity for the quickly growing urban middle class.

Usury, interest and profit stopped being theologically problematic. And thus, in the new age, reformed Christianity walked hand in hand with capitalism.

The purpose of financial instruments is, in varying ways, to manage economic risk. Move it away from people who can't weather it to others who can. The olive crop that year could have been meagre, the harvest could have burned or been visited by frost. Thales took that risk for the farmers, and therefore he was able to profit later. The financial markets are a paradox in the sense that they can't make a profit without taking risks. At the same time, they collapse when too many risks are taken.

In 1997 rock legend David Bowie needed money. He had turned fifty and finally wanted to buy out his former manager Tony Defries, who still had the rights to some of Bowie's earnings even though they had parted ways years before.

Bowie was certainly not poor. Money was coming in all the time. From 'Space Oddity', 'Rebel Rebel', 'Jean Genie' and

'Ziggy Stardust'. And money would continue to flow in over the next decades. Royalties from the twenty-five albums and 287 songs he had recorded.

But he wanted to have the money now.

He offered the market a so-called Bowie Bond – a new form of financial product. Money was time and time was money. And you could apparently twist and play with the relationship.

Bowie sold his future income from music that was already recorded and composed. Those who bought Bowie Bonds received in return a part of his future royalties in perpetuity, and David Bowie could sign for 87 million pounds immediately.

He no longer had money coming in year after year – instead he received one lump sum.

It was not only other artists that started thinking along similar lines around this time – American banks did too. Just as Bowie would have had millions trickling in slowly over several decades, the banks had billions loaned out to people who had bought houses. This money was coming in because people were paying back their loans.

Why not then sell these loans – just like Bowie had sold his royalties?

A bank loaned maybe 100,000 dollars each to 10,000 American families. That was one billion dollars that the bank would get back over the next twenty-five years. Now the bank created a paper that said whoever owns this paper would have a right to money from the loans. The bank then sold the paper to someone else (for example, a pension fund) and as if by magic got back a new, cool billion to loan to 100,000 new families.

It was magical. You lend one billion, sell the loan on and get one billion. But the only thing you've really sold is a bundle of debts. More money. Less risk. Everyone wins. This fundamentally changed the operations of many bankers. Of course, the problem was that the risk was still there. Somewhere in the system.

It was likely that David Bowie's songs would continue to generate money when he created his bonds in 1997 and received his 87 million. That was the sum that his future royalty payments for his music were valued at. Because how could anyone in 1997 have predicted what a huge phenomenon music downloads would be? Or how much they would decrease an artist's earnings? We know this today. But that isn't David Bowie's problem.

The people who bought the bonds – it's their problem.

Once, the bank bore the consequences if a borrower defaulted on his mortgage payments. Naturally, banks were more careful with lending then. Now the relationship had been turned on its head. Banks started to care less and less about who they lent money to. They were selling the loan on anyway. The more money a bank lent, the more loans it had to sell – and the more money they earned it.

The credit-rating businesses that were supposed to appraise this type of financial product should have seen the risks. But they were paid by the same banks that had created the securities they were being asked to grade. And the credit-rating businesses were companies in a market. If a bank didn't like its score from one company it could go to another one. Furthermore, the banks and credit-rating businesses used the same economic models. Models that built on the idea that all people were like economic man. It was quite simply impossible that house prices would fall uncontrollably. The market couldn't be wrong, and so these papers were, in other words, 'secure'.

The American Federal Reserve kept interest rates at a historic low instead of doing something about the situation.

The standard of living of the American middle class had increased very little since the 1970s. For politicians of all stripes, it was important that the middle classes, in spite of the widening rifts, felt like winners. What else is the United States if not the story of a middle class that was becoming better off? The dream of having your own home became the solution. Every American family should have the opportunity – not be able to afford, but have the opportunity – to buy their own home. The idea was built on being able to sell time. If house prices went up, why couldn't debts increase at the same rate? The ever-increasing value of the house was security enough. Your income mattered less, or not at all.

Between 1997 and 2006 housing prices in the USA increased 124%. When the bubble was at its worst, 160,000 people were buying houses each week. This was the biggest economic bubble in the history of mankind.

Banks lent money to people who couldn't pay it back. What is more, they lent far too much money and ultimately they themselves bought back many of the loans because the credit-rating agencies had said these papers were so safe. When the bubble burst the banks sat there without money and with papers that turned out to be worthless. Papers that, on top of everything, were spread all over the world. And no one wanted to touch them.

On 15 September 2008, the investment bank Lehman Brothers crashed. That was the starting shot. The American banks dragged the global economy down with them.

Speculation and financial madness has led to economic catastrophes as far back as people can remember. 'This time is different,' we say time and time again, according to Carmen M. Reinhart and Kenneth S. Rogoff in *This Time is Different: Eight Centuries of Financial Folly*. Speculation arises when our collective fantasy locks its sights on something that we think is completely new and unique. We create value by creating objects that are different from ourselves, then we try to bridge that distance.

When it becomes known that people are earning a lot of money in a certain market, more people invest there. It drives up the prices, and the more prices go up, the more people invest. And of course, the more they invest, the more prices go up. Even when people start to see what's happening it doesn't seem to have a significant effect. They continue to throw money straight into the bubble.

Inevitably it gets to the point when everything turns and someone starts shouting 'sell'. The panic spreads, and everyone rushes to the exit at the same time. Prices fall just as quickly, often more quickly, than they rose. So even more rush towards the exit, and prices fall even more. Exaggerated optimism turns to exaggerated pessimism. Everyone is looking for the pot of gold at the end of the rainbow. And then it goes up in smoke. When you think you can make something of nothing, it's very hard to stop.

Economic value appears and vanishes in collective hallucinations. Faster and faster. Capital flows freely over borders and at the speed of light. It no longer resides in factories or where things are made or where natural resources are extracted. When financiers chase profits, they don't compete with each other for customers like a service-based company might or develop rival products as tech companies do. Financiers chase profits in the form of speculation itself. And with great fluctuations comes easy money, greater risks and greater losses. It's bet on a bet on a bet.

As Gordon Gekko says in Oliver Stone's 1987 film *Wall Street*, it has become a zero-sum game. Money is neither lost nor made, just moved from one perception to the next. 'The illusion has become real. And the more real it becomes, the more desperately they want it,' he states crassly.

Even Mephistopheles in Goethe's *Faust* understood this. He was the Devil's representative, after all, waiting for the opportunity to get a hold of Faust's soul and take it down to hell with him. Faust himself just wanted to be happy. According to Swiss economist Hans Christoph Binswanger, Faust is representative of modern man: through science and knowledge he seeks to subjugate nature and build up a new economic realm. He wants freedom and prosperity, all the pleasure, all the knowledge and everything that makes you beg and pray that this moment will never end. Is that too much to ask?

Today abstract algorithms are increasingly replacing the broker's contribution to the financial markets. Computers buy and sell automatically according to mathematical models. Brokers in sweaty contrast collar shirts and red suspenders who shout and wave at numbers on big screens like in the movie *Wall Street*: soon they won't exist, even if their fashion sense unfortunately might prevail. Instead there are specialized companies with ultra-fast computer systems that carry out automated mass trade based on advanced mathematics. The big banks don't even live on Wall Street any more. They have moved to spaces better suited to their large computer systems. The biggest resources buy the biggest computer. The fastest wins. They try to earn money on how the prices fluctuate from second to second in various markets. Sometimes things go wrong in this faceless universe – an order of 10.8 billion dollars can become 10.8 million dollars due to a technical error. The so-called algorithms could go crazy and run amok – buy up the whole universe before we have a chance to blink. Security systems are therefore well-oiled and the manoeuvres are well-practised. This type of trade happens 1,000 times faster than the blink of an eye. A technical error in the financial fantasy could cause the next big crash. It could happen in minutes.

The wake of a hyperventilating global stock market could cause millions of people to lose their jobs. Millions of unemployed people in turn could create a deficit in countries' finances, and governments could be forced to, with a grim expression, cut into care for the elderly. But the number of elderly who need to be fed and turned over and to have their hands held wouldn't change. Fewer nursing assistants would have to do the same amount of work. Backs and joints might not be able to hold out. And so the cost of a mistake in a bet about a split-second price change over in the financial casino can travel all the way down to the normal left knee of a female nursing assistant. A knee that neither Adam Smith nor the chieftains of the financial world ever took into consideration.

*

When the crisis became a fact in the autumn of 2008, Alan Greenspan, chief of the American Federal Reserve, was interrogated in Congress. The democrat Henry Waxman wondered:

– You found that your view of the world, your ideology, was not right, it was not working?

– That's precisely the reason I was shocked because I'd been going for 40 years or so with considerable evidence that it was working exceptionally well.

Economics has become a logic and a game in its own universe. All people everywhere were seen as economic man: individual expressions of one and the same infallible economic consciousness. And everything that happens is rational.

Prosperity was created somewhere in another financial universe, almost entirely disconnected from what you did with your mortgage or from how a business was actually faring. Value could increase anyway. It all happened on another level – gold appeared and vanished through mysterious processes. As if economics and the markets didn't have anything to do with us any more. What we produce, how we work, what we invent and need.

Technological changes have always transformed markets. When money becomes increasingly abstract – first as deerskin and metal pieces and finally as bundles of loans that are bought and sold – more and more people start to think it is within reach. The potential for prosperity is enormous, but so are the risks. Especially if we don't succeed in keeping a handle on what prosperity was about to begin with.

Regardless of our ability to create computer systems that

can buy and sell the whole world to themselves twelve times over in 300 microseconds. Regardless of the seductive elegance of mathematics, we can't get away from the fact that at its core economics is based on the human body. Bodies that work, bodies that need care, bodies that create other bodies. Bodies that are born, age and die. Bodies that are sexed. Bodies that need help through many phases of life.

And a society that can support them.

CHAPTER EIGHT

*In which we see that men are also not like economic
man*

Since the 1950s psychologists and economists have been
systematically testing the assumptions standard economic
theory makes about people. They have conducted experiments
on thought and decision-making processes and studied MRI
scans of the brain. They have asked themselves over and over
again, who is this economic man?

The first full-frontal attack on economic man was
published in 1979. Two Israeli researchers, Daniel Kahneman
and Amos Tversky, were able to demonstrate that, contrary to
what economists asserted, our decisions weren't objective or
rational at all. Kahneman was awarded the 2002 Nobel Prize
in Economic Sciences, and one would think that this would
have been the end of economic man.

Kahneman and Tversky established that we care more
about risk avoidance than about maximizing profit. We often
arrive at very different conclusions based on how a problem
is described, and in contrast to the world of economic man,
context matters. Also, our preferences aren't constant, but
rather are impacted by how they are measured. If we own an

item, we seem to automatically believe it's more valuable, and we perceive that it is more unpleasant to lose 100 pounds than it is fun to win as much. We generally prefer for things to stay as they are, even if we don't benefit from it.

Above all, we put the well-being of others ahead of our own in many situations. Even when it represents a loss for us.

Real people tip in restaurants they'll never visit again. Economic man doesn't. The waitress will never be able to exact revenge by putting a fly in his soup, so he pockets his money and leaves without giving it a second thought.

Real people are often willing to cooperate. Economic man only cooperates when it benefits him. He also doesn't care if he appears to have an unfair advantage in a situation – he just wants to win.

For the rest of us, these things matter.

It also matters if people bargain with each other face to face. If we look someone in the eye, we are more careful. For economic man it's six of one, half a dozen of the other. And moreover, irrelevant. All situations are the same: an exchange between one or more calculating individuals. There is no context. Everything is whole and nothing is half, and yes, it is in fact a competition.

In reality we are not rational, selfish individuals. Men as well as women, children as well as adults, young as well as old. We are often thoughtful. Often confused. Often selfless. Often worried. Often illogical. And above all, not one of us is an island.

Our stories about the economy aren't separate, but rather they shape the economy when it's on the way up and when it's on the way down. We hear how others grow rich and how companies turn record profits, it doesn't matter if it's true. It makes us think that everything will sort itself out. And so it becomes true. To a degree. Because we start spending as if it were true.

In the same way, horror stories about free-falling market values and panicked brokers shouting 'sell' make us hold on more tightly to our savings. In that way, we also contribute to the deepening of the recession. Our feelings create our stories – and our stories become movements on the market.

If everyone you know is prepared to pay 250,000 pounds for a new apartment, the dark headlines about the ongoing property bubble won't seem as frightening. You ask the estate agent to raise your offer by another 10,000 pounds. A boom has been described as an effect of collective optimism that spreads through society. Our collective feelings can't be turned off. If we had had an economic theory that took them into account, we could have avoided a number of problems.

And understood something about ourselves.

Economic behaviour is in many ways driven by emotion – not by reason. And it is collective – not individualist. No one who watched the global economy collapse in 2008 could believe that it was well thought through or a result of the kind of informed economic decision-making that we are told is the only kind we are capable of.

Already in the 1930s John Maynard Keynes wrote about the feelings, impulses and more or less enthusiastic misunderstandings that both drive and topple economies. After the financial crisis of 2008 these ideas were revisited. Economists George Akerlof and Robert Shiller believed that we forgot about this part of Keynes's explanation for the crisis of the '30s. Even though we embraced other parts of his theories, we held on to the idea of the consistently rational person – incapable of seeing the collective or emotional aspects of the market.

But if economic man isn't like us, who is he then?

Expectations of justice and cooperation usually impact on people's behaviour. We expect that others will cooperate and share. If they act unfairly, we refuse to take part – even if it is to our disadvantage.

Psychologists conducted an experiment with nursery school children and with students in the second and sixth grades to see if they were like economic man. The students who were older than seven years reacted to injustice – just like adults. The younger children, on the other hand, behaved just like economic man.

When the five-year-olds were supposed to take a position on the offer of splitting a sum of money, they didn't care if it was fairly split – they just wanted to have as much as possible. If they were given only a small sum, it was better than nothing. They gladly grabbed anything they could get their hands on. Just like economic man. But five-year-olds don't run the global economy.

Or is that exactly how it is?

The researchers who conducted the study established that from the age of seven we begin to take factors like justice into consideration. The economic-man phase is a passing phase, or at least so it seemed in a simplified experiment using games in a laboratory. In all likelihood, even five-year-olds are more complex in real-world situations.

There is no human society that is driven only by greed and

fear, self-interest and rationality. It would never work. The economist and philosopher Amartya Sen has illustrated this with the following exchange:

'Where is the railway station?' asks the stranger. 'There,' says the villager, pointing in the other direction, at the post office, 'and would you please post this letter for me on the way?'

'Of course,' he says, determined to open the envelope and check whether it contains something valuable.

That's not how the world works.

The equations about why economic man does what he does are relatively complicated mathematics. At the same time, psychological research shows that real people don't choose the most rational option in a situation particularly often. Often we don't even understand what 'the most rational option' would be. And these results come from simplified experiments using play-money in a laboratory. Even then we don't succeed in being rational. Out in the real world things are infinitely more complicated. How can anyone have an overview of everything? Weigh each possibility against the other, manage to calculate and maximize gain?

Are we even capable of being like economic man?

The neoliberal economist Milton Friedman's famous challenge to this kind of criticism is about billiards. Picture a skilled billiard player. He doesn't necessarily know the laws of physics. He plays as if he knew them. And that's all we need to know.

Now we can predict his behaviour by creating a model. In the model we simply assume that the billiard player knows the laws of physics. That might not be true. But the model will work anyway because the billiard player plays as if he knows the laws of physics.

People are, in other words, perhaps not like economic man. Still we act, according to Friedman, as if we were. Therefore, a model based on economic man can predict what people will do and what will happen in the economy.

According to this logic, economists shouldn't be judged on how correct their view of people is. Economists should be judged on how well their conclusions conform to the de facto actions of people in the market.

But predicting the market is, in all honesty, not something that economics has done particularly well. When the financial crisis hit in the autumn of 2008, Queen Elizabeth II visited the London School of Economics. The gathered experts described the ongoing crisis. The Queen looked surprised: 'Why did nobody see this coming?' she wondered. And that was a good question.

Harvard professor and American diplomat John Kenneth Galbraith once quipped that God created economists to give astrologists a better reputation, and he was himself one of the world's most celebrated economists.

The Nobel prize-winning American economist Robert Lucas felt compelled to answer the Queen. In the *Economist* magazine he explained that economists didn't predict the crisis because they had predicted that this kind of event couldn't be predicted.

The question is whether the Queen was any the wiser for that.

*

Today the market drives the world economy to a greater degree than ever before. And we have in the last decades listened to economists more than ever. This period has nevertheless been a time of crises. The 1987 American stock market crash. Japan's economic meltdown. The 1994 Mexican financial crisis. The crisis after the hedge fund Long Term Capital failed in 1998. (One year after Myron Scholes and Robert C. Merton were awarded their Nobel prize for their theories about why Long Term Capital would never fail.) The Russian financial crisis that same year. The Asian crisis. The IT crash at the turn of the millennium. And finally, 2008's global financial crisis. The worst crisis since the Great Depression. For all but a handful of economists this was a complete shock.

After the fall of the Soviet Union, the International Monetary Fund and the United States Department of the Treasury pushed through privatization in Russia with record speed. A number of economists tried to turn the country from a planned economy to a market economy in the space of days – not years. If you tore away the layers of communism, a country of rational economic individuals would peer through, they reasoned, and the people would start building a vibrant capitalist society as if they had never done anything differently. Russia's institutions, history, division of wealth and social norms weren't thought to matter. There was no reason to get involved in the details. The economic principles were universal. The doctrines should work regardless. Beyond all context, all history, all cohesion and all the circumstances that determine what we normally call 'existence'. In the models there was only one world. Human nature. Economic man.

The result is well known: a small group of oligarchs

quickly took control of Russia's assets. Suddenly the State couldn't even pay out pensions, and at the same time the country's resources were being sold with gusto. Money was moved to bank accounts in Switzerland and Cyprus. The whole thing seemed more like organized crime than organized markets. What was left was a country with a lower standard of living than before the reforms and millions of people who wondered if this was really the point of democracy. No, thank you, in that case, they said and elected Vladimir Putin as president on promises of stability and resurrected pride.

Each year of the 1990s, per capita incomes fell in Russia. Even the Ukraine went through a similar development. Poland, which paid no mind to the advice of the International Monetary Fund, fared significantly better.

Making a capitalist economy communist is 'like making fish soup from an aquarium', said union leader Lech Wałęsa, later to become president. The difficulty lay in performing the trick the other way around.

The market is far from a harmoniously ticking piece of clockwork, an inevitable consequence of rational, human individuals following a single path through life. It's more complicated than that. The market's distinguishing feature, if anything, is one of incredible pressure to change. Without sentimentality it sweeps away old companies, old technologies and everything else that it doesn't have a use for; in many cases, people. The market isn't very considerate. That's why it can drive development to such a degree, but it can also destroy development for the same reason – and with the same power. The market is terribly effective in some areas and terribly ineffective in others. It is everything but mechanical, simple and inevitable.

Economists who believe in economic man usually assert that their picture of mankind may be incomplete, but it's complete enough to be useful. Undeniably, economists have taught us things about how the world works that have helped us to make it better – if they say that economic man can help them, why not believe them? Why not simplify the picture of man and the market? Simplification is a tool. We use it in many areas.

The earth is round, we say, for example. But it's not. The earth is an ellipsis. And ribbed with mountains, valleys and melting polar ice caps.

But even if we say that the earth is round, we would never be able to navigate our vessels (or, for that matter, cruise missiles) using maps drawn as if the world were a perfect sphere. When we draw maps, we try to measure the earth's irregularities and then take them into consideration in some way. We let economic man, on the other hand, be. The models created around him are used as a foundation to guide the global economy and are prescribed to poor countries with problems. Here you go, now get it together! In spite of the fact that we have known for over thirty years that in the best case, economic man is a simplification – in the worst case, a hallucination.

Today he continues to define what economic logic is. It's still this picture of mankind that is taught on university foundation courses in economics – not to mention in popular science books that apply the market to increasingly large portions of our lives. Economic man dominates, even though for years research has been able to show that he has very little to do with reality. We continue to be seduced. And he continues to insist that we are all like him. Whether we know it or not. And whatever we do.

A man climbs up a church tower and crows like a rooster. You'd say he's mad. But what do you know about that? Some people skydive, others climb the Himalayas – that's also dangerous. You don't try to kill your girlfriend with a lettuce leaf. Then you'd be mad. You try to murder your girlfriend with a knife. Then you plead madness. But economic man knows better. He knows you're always rational, no matter what you're pleading.

If you put a gun to the head of an alcoholic and tell him not to drink, he'll put down his glass. It has, therefore, always been an option for him to stop drinking. He just wasn't choosing to. He simply didn't have a reason to. Until now. Who are you to call someone mad? Who are you to say that someone doesn't know what is for their own good?

Once there was a man who lived with eleven swans in his flat. He had caught them in the park at night and carried them home, one by one, wrapped in a blanket. One of the swans had a broken wing. The man fixed it with a rubber band and a bit of masking tape. When the police came to retrieve the birds, the man was sad. Was there something wrong with him? Or did he simply have, as economic man would say, a preference for swans?

Some people wash their hands 200 times a day, others refuse to make left-hand turns when driving. There are some people who can watch sports for ten hours straight. There are those who scrub the bathroom floor for fifteen hours. If you are worried that Arsenal will lose, you devote yourself to worrying. If you are afraid of bacteria, you devote yourself to them. There is one logic. One rationality. If you feel really bad, you kill yourself. The meaning of it all isn't found in the big picture. It's locked in a container that shouldn't be opened. Many mental patients are convinced that everyone other than them is mad. My compulsive episodes and rituals are normal reactions to abnormal circumstances. They turn off the lights in the ward, you cry out in anguish and the empty sound that comes out of your mouth is also a form of demand. The world continues to turn in the track that it carves out for itself. It's hell's own carousel. You have to get more out of it than you put in, anything else is the definition of pointlessness. Even in one single army that marches in one single direction, you are always alone. One logic, one world and you die your own death.

This is the world we cling to.

CHAPTER NINE

*In which economic incentives aren't shown to be as
uncomplicated as we might think*

Once there was a man and a woman who owned a very special
goose. Every morning when they woke, the goose had laid
an egg made of pure gold. At first, the couple didn't understand what the unusual eggs were. Heavy as lead and much
bigger. Eventually they realized what the eggs were made of.
The couple started to sell them one by one, and in time they
became very rich.

'Imagine,' said the man to the woman one day, 'if there
were some way we could get at all the gold inside the goose.'
'Yes,' the woman answered, 'then we wouldn't have to wait for
her to lay every morning.'

So the couple went to the farmyard and slaughtered the
bird. But when they eagerly cut up the dead goose, to their
horror they didn't find any golden eggs. Just blood, tendons,
feathers and innards. On the inside, the goose was like any
other bird. And there were not going to be any more golden
eggs. The goose who laid them was dead.

*

There is no language on earth that is taken as seriously as that of economics.

'Improved growth projections lead to more robust public finances.' 'Normalization of the market.' 'Let the market decide.' 'Level the playing field.' 'Lower the thresholds.' 'Make the tough decisions.' 'Blunt instruments to stimulate demand.' 'Improved forecast for productivity.' 'Less favoured currency development.' 'Competition-driven market.' 'Very strong marginal effects.'

A language of pure necessity. We all know what has to be done, just not whether we'll be re-elected after we've done it.

The ecstasy of reason.

The first markets emerged around settlements and between villages. It was considered important to keep commerce outside the human community. The logic of the market to buy and sell shouldn't be mixed in with the rest of society. It should keep itself on the periphery, and people performed magical rituals to keep the boundaries between places of trade and themselves holy and stable. Places of trade were marked with a stone, and the market's logic was supposed to be kept within the border that the stone indicated.

Many thousands of years have passed since then, and the logic of the market has flooded the banks. Upwards. Outwards. Inwards. To refer to 'economics' has become synonymous with referring to 'rationality'. To buy, sell and compete is held up as an image of society as a whole. Politics is analysed in this way, as is the law, love – our whole existence. For every transaction we make there is someone to tell us how it relates to economic ideas of self-interest, competition and achieving the greatest satisfaction for the lowest cost. Oscar Wilde's cynic knew 'the price of everything and the value of nothing', but no one told him that value was measured by demand.

The market hasn't just moved into the centres of the largest metropolises – buildings raised in its honour downright define the big cities: New York, Shanghai, Tokyo, London, Kuala Lumpur. The silhouettes of metropolitan areas everywhere are dominated by the skyscrapers of the banking and finance sectors. We have never before been able to build so high or create on such a large scale, but on the tops of skyscrapers we have to place safety nets – otherwise people will hurl themselves through the clouds, towards death, 100 floors down, right into the street.

At the same time as economic man has grown and taken over the world, the markets still seem to need our incantations. Maybe now more than ever. We are constantly concerned about their welfare. The market can be positive, worried, over-heated, happy and upset – a remarkable beast full of feelings. Its inner life is so rich that some of the world's most prestigious newspapers are dedicated to following its every fluctuation.

Sometimes it thinks and contemplates:

'The market ignored how prices were expected to rise.' 'Yesterday the market struggled to make a decision.' 'The market interpreted the government's decision as it's not going to devalue.' 'The market's quick response took everyone by surprise.' 'The market drew its own conclusion.'

Sometimes it's stubborn and unhappy:

'The market was little impressed by the government's measure.' 'The market is still far from convinced that Italy means business.' 'The market was rather disappointed by the German Bundesbank.'

It can be aggressive and violent:

'The Greek government found itself engaged in full-scale war with the market.' 'The US might let the market knock down the dollar.' 'The market smelled blood.' 'The Central Bank still has some ammunition left.' 'We have to convince the market that we mean business!'

But it can also feel bad:

'Last week the market was tense.' 'The decline of the pound has upset the market.' 'The market is still reeling after the hard knock.' 'The market's nervousness was probably the fault of finance minister Anders Borg.' 'The market was confused by his comments.' 'The market's primary feeling was insecurity.' 'The market has gone into spasms.' The market is depressed.' 'Yesterday Portugal tried to calm the market.'

When the market is unusually upset (clinically depressed or in some form of free-falling anxiety), then society has to make an offering to it. Great sums of money. The economy must be 'stimulated'. People, the State, or both must consume more to keep the market going. It's expensive, but the alternative is far too frightening to even consider. Consumption becomes sacred blood – at once clean, unclean, beautiful, disgusting and holy.

'With all the talk about how to stimulate it, you'd think that the economy is a giant clitoris,' wrote the American journalist Barbara Ehrenreich. Of course, when you think about it, the economy isn't nearly as complicated as the female body.

But it does take a sensitive touch.

The economy is, on one hand, the clear voice of reason (ideally expressed through complex mathematics). On the other hand, it's all about the emotional life of the market. A wild and unruly emotional life that is described as such with thousands of nuances – up and down the columns of the *Financial Times*, *Dagens Industri* and the *Wall Street Journal*.

While we describe the market as if it has human emotions, we increasingly describe ourselves as if we don't have human emotions. As if we were empty goods or companies on, that's right, a market.

'I have to think about my personal brand.' 'You have to invest in our relationship.' 'It's fun to be on the market again.' 'I owe you more than I can give in our relationship.' 'You have to get better at selling yourself.' 'Children are an investment in our future.' 'He doesn't want to take on the emotional cost.' 'She has passed her expiration date.'

While human language is used to describe the market, the language of the market increasingly is used to describe people.

The economy has become us, and we have become the economy.

In the book *Spousonomics: Using Economics to Master Love, Marriage, and Dirty Dishes*, Paula Szuchman and Jenny Anderson promise to improve our romantic relationships with the help of economic principles.

Szuchman and Anderson see marriage as a speculative business, and the book's purpose is to help you learn how to maximize your returns. It's the market's logic applied all the way to the bedroom. The starting point is that every romantic relationship is its own little economy: two rational economic individuals under one roof. Marriage is a business with limited resources that have to be distributed effectively for it to be fruitful. And according to Szuchman and Anderson, the market's principles can help us with all of it: the fights about the laundry, about the children and about not having sex with each other any more.

They use Howard as an example.

When Howard comes home to his family in the evening, he frequently flies into a rage. Toys and tricycles lay scattered everywhere and Howard loses it. Nothing helps. Howard shouts and nothing can calm him down. Every single time.

Until his wife Jen starts applying *Spousonomics*.

People are selfish and react to incentives, say the standard theories of economics. When training a dog, you command it to sit, and if the dog does what you say, you give it a treat. The treat is an incentive – the dog sitting is the desirable behaviour. Economic man always reacts well to incentives, a lightning-quick calculator calculates what he'll gain in every situation.

According to these theories, people's behaviour can always be traced back to what they gain and don't gain from a situation. Howard's outbursts aren't desirable behaviour. They irritate his wife and frighten his children. Therefore Howard must be given an incentive to stop acting this way.

It has to be of sufficient worth for him not to fly into a rage.

Jen creates a system of incentives. If Howard doesn't get angry three nights in a row – then she'll have sex with him. And rightly: Howard soon stops kicking up a fuss. Proof that an economic trade-off works, chirp Szuchman and Anderson.

Back to the '50s, someone else might say.

Spousonomics keeps quiet about the fact that by doing this Jen has changed the fundaments of her marriage. When Jen implemented economic incentives she simultaneously killed the adult sexuality of her marriage.

Sexuality has been turned from a place to play, an invitation to come and be with another person, into a system of rewards. Howard has been turned from a man into some sort of bizarre child who has to be fed with sex in order to keep calm. And Jen's body has stopped being a part of her. It has become a tool, something she uses to keep her man happy.

It's an age-old story, no matter how many economic equations it's dressed up in.

The thing about economic incentives is that they are not as uncomplicated as we think.

Just over a century ago bubonic plague broke out in Hanoi. To counteract the spread of the illness, municipal rat-catchers were employed. They were supposed to kill the rats, especially those in the city's sewer system, and soon they were working busy days. The rats multiplied quicker than the rat-catchers could handle, and in spite of killing thousands every day, the rat population didn't seem to be getting any smaller.

The French colonial power enlisted the help of the general public. For each rat tail that was brought to the authorities, a reward was given. Initially, the programme seemed to be very successful. Thousands of rat tails were brought in every day, but the authorities soon suspected mischief. The streets appeared to be full of tail-less live rats. And people had even started to raise the animals for the sole purpose of cutting off their tails and getting remunerated by the authorities.

The problem with many things is that you get exactly what you pay for, and it never turns out as expected – precisely because you get what you pay for.

The rat-catching programme in Hanoi was terminated.

*

At a day care centre in Israel the staff had long had a problem with stressed parents not being able to leave work on time. Day after day the staff had to work overtime. Two economists conducted a study of the problem.

To deal with the late pick-ups, the day care centre implemented fees. Parents who picked their children up late were charged. But this resulted in the parents picking up the children even later. How was this possible?

When the day care centre implemented late-fees, they mistakenly killed the thing that made parents try to pick their children up on time. Their duty to. The feeling of knowing you were supposed to arrive at five o'clock, otherwise you'd be inconveniencing the staff. By implementing fees, the day care centre, without thinking about it, put a price on late pick-ups, and if there is a price, then you can pay it, and so you can do the right thing.

Parents started to see the fees as a charge for an extra service. The moral imperative died. The relationship between parents and personnel changed. The initial motivation wasn't related to money. And if you make it about money, you change the parameters of the situation.

When you offer a passer-by compensation for helping you unload a sofa from a lorry, they are less inclined to do it. People want to help. But if you introduce money into the equation, you lose this motive.

Then it becomes about performing a service in exchange for payment, and in this situation people have been shown to be significantly less interested.

In their standard models, economists usually assume the

more motives the better. One plus one is two. And two is always more than one. In the same way, two reasons to do something are better than one. That's how economic man works. If he wants to pick his children up from day care on time because he prefers not to inconvenience the staff, so be it. There is nothing that prevents him from reacting to a monetary incentive. The rest of us are more complicated. Not because economic incentives don't affect us. But because they do.

The teacher who earns more money if the children earn better marks on standardized tests will ensure higher marks on that exam – but not necessarily better-educated students.

The director who gets a hundred grand bonus if the company's stock goes up will make sure that the company's stock goes up, but he won't necessarily be doing the best thing for the company in the long run.

When incentives are to be implemented, one often looks for something that is easy to measure and that can be used as an index for what one wants improved. Good results on standardized tests are a measure of the students' knowledge – just like the value of the stock is a measure of how well the business is doing.

But what often happens is that people try to work around the incentive. Teachers start teaching how one earns good marks on the exam. Not knowledge. The CEO starts making decisions that make the stock rise in the short term. Not that strengthen the company beyond the next quarterly report.

The problem with economic incentives is not that they don't work but that even though they do, they often change the nature of a situation. Sometimes this doesn't matter. Like when a charity started offering free vaccinations in rural India. In spite of the vaccines being available to all, still eight out of ten children were unvaccinated. The organization started experimenting with ways to entice parents to vaccinate their children. The most effective way seemed to be to offer them a few free portions of lentil stew. Parents who before hadn't seen the point of vaccinating their children now had a reason to do so, and the percentage of vaccinations increased. In many situations, economic incentives work wonderfully. However, people aren't isolated players who chase every carrot and perform for every whip. We don't exist in a world where everything is economically calculated. If you introduce an economic incentive, you risk, like in the Israeli day care centre, killing the thing that was holding the situation together.

An economic study was done in Switzerland before the country held one of its many referendums. It was about whether or not they should store nuclear waste, and the scientists were interested in knowing how people thought through this issue.

They went door to door with their questionnaire: could people imagine a nuclear waste facility in the neighbourhood? Fifty per cent answered 'yes'.

Certainly people thought it seemed dangerous and certainly it would decrease the value of their houses. This they didn't like. But that facility has to go somewhere. So if the authorities want to put it here – then they felt they had a responsibility. As Swiss citizens.

When people, on the other hand, were asked if they would consider the facility if they were compensated for their trouble with a relatively large annual sum – the equivalent of six weeks' work for an average worker – then suddenly only 25% answered yes. They wanted to be good citizens, but it wasn't about that any more. The monetary incentive killed the true incentive.

The goose that lays the golden eggs is often something other than what we think it is.

That's why we risk her life.

We implement an economic incentive with the belief that economic forces are what drive us. Then the incentive happens to push away all other driving forces. Economic man runs into a situation and succeeds in simultaneously knocking over moral, emotional and cultural considerations that in retrospect had been incredibly important for the functioning of the economy and its development. Defined in this way, the market's principles don't just have a hard time explaining the most important things.

They also risk ruining the most important things.

CHAPTER TEN

*In which we see that you aren't selfish just because
you want more money*

Nancy Folbre, a feminist professor of economics, often tells
this tale:

Once there were a number of goddesses who decided to
hold a competition, a sort of Olympics for the countries of
the world. This wasn't an ordinary race with a fixed distance
where whoever reaches the finish line first wins a medal. It was
a competition to see which society could move its members
forward as a whole. The starting shot was fired and nation
number one quickly took the lead.

This nation encouraged each of its citizens to run as best
they could, as fast as they could towards an unknown finish line
– and they assumed that the track couldn't be too long. They
started running very fast and soon children and the elderly
lagged behind. None of the other runners stopped to help
them. They were overjoyed with how fast they were running
and couldn't spare the time. But as the race continued, even
they began to tire. By and by, almost all of the runners were
ailing and injured – and there was nobody else to take their
place.

Nation number two had a different strategy. This society sent all of its young men forth and told the women to take up the rear. The women would carry the children and take care of the elderly. This meant that the men could run incredibly quickly. The women were close by and could help them when they grew tired. This appeared at first to be an excellent system. Soon, it was plagued by conflict. The women felt that their efforts were at least as important as the men's. If they hadn't had to carry the children, they could have run just as fast, they reasoned. The men refused to take their point. And what had seemed like a winning strategy lost momentum. Ever more energy was spent on conflicts, negotiations and fights.

Now the attention shifted to nation number three. This one had been moving relatively slowly. But when the goddesses looked in its direction they saw that this country moved at a much steadier pace than the others. Here participants were expected to both run and take care of those less able. Men and women were equally encouraged to take the lead and everyone took turns taking care of the children and the infirm. Both speed and contribution to the whole were valued, and this shared responsibility created solidarity among the people. Clearly this nation won the contest. It's a rather sweet story.

Every society must in some way create a structure for how to care for other people, otherwise neither the economy nor anything else will work. 'How do you get your dinner?' is the fundamental question of economics, and even if Adam Smith wrote that the answer was self-interest, his mother had made sure food was on the table every night and cared for him when he had a fever.

Without care children can't grow, the sick won't get healthy, Adam Smith can't write and the old can't live. Being cared for by others is the medium through which we learn cooperation, empathy, respect, self-discipline and thoughtfulness. These are fundamental life skills.

Economic science wanted to 'conserve love'. Love was supposed to be saved by being excluded, and driving forces like thoughtfulness, empathy and care were pushed out of the analysis. They weren't considered traits that created prosperity.

The one was done for money. The other out of thoughtfulness. And never the twain shall meet.

Equally important was that the same thing happened in the inverse: prosperity and money were left out of conversations about thoughtfulness, empathy and care. Perhaps it is this omission that best explains why women's economic standing today is so much worse than men's.

'Money is human happiness in the abstract,' wrote the philosopher Arthur Schopenhauer. 'He, then, who is no longer capable of enjoying human happiness in the concrete, devotes his heart entirely to money.' Money is frozen desire, not a desire for anything special, but rather a symbol of the fulfilment of desire in general.

We worship money. But at some level we think it's a little unseemly. Like most desires. Especially in women.

Traditionally care work has been conducted in the home, which was seen as the place where a man could return after a hard day in the cold, impersonal, wage-earning world. Sink down into woman's soft kingdom of emotion, morality, sensuality and finely crocheted lace curtains.

Here, the man wasn't a cog in a machine that would be given economic incentives for acting in a desirable way. Here, he could take a holiday from the market, and allow himself to become a better person under the mild gaze of a woman. A woman's duty wasn't just to balance a man's life through care and empathy and to put him in touch with the aspects of the human experience that he couldn't accept in himself. She was also supposed to create balance in society.

As long as her soft world complemented the demands of the market, we as a species wouldn't tip over into unfettered greed and competition. Woman, through her care and empathy, gave meaning to man's struggle in the workforce. This was her economic function. So went the tale at the start of the Victorian era, when capitalism as we know it today grew large enough to start telling stories about itself.

Even when care work was moved out of the home and into the hospital, day care centre and nursing home, the dichotomy of love and money remained. To take care of others was something one did because one was a good person – that is, female. Not because one wanted to have a career or earn a living.

Many of the first nurses were nuns. They had sworn an oath of poverty. The nursing corps was otherwise made up of young women who were waiting to get married. They had no family to take care of and eventually would be taken care of by a man, they didn't need to make a living from their work. Moreover, a nurse's calling was noble and important, it was reasoned. That's why it shouldn't pay.

For men, the opposite logic is applied: work that is important for society should pay well, we think. If my large bank goes bankrupt, the whole economy will collapse – that's why I should be given a half-a-million-pound bonus. But this logic doesn't apply to women. And because care workers are mainly women, this logic doesn't apply to that kind of job either.

Whether women work in the care sector because the wages are low or whether wages are low because women work there is a question that can't be answered. But we know that a big reason for economic inequality between men and women is that women to a much greater extent work with care. And nursing and care are economically undervalued largely because of the dichotomy between love and money.

The founder of the modern nursing profession, Florence Nightingale, was born in Florence in 1820 to British parents. They named her after the Tuscan city on the river Arno where she had come into the world, and because they were well-off she had the opportunity to receive an education.

Florence had a deep faith and believed from early on that God had called to her to become a nurse. Her mother balked at this. Nursing was a career with a bad reputation that was managed by poor women. In spite of the family's protests, Florence learned the art and science of nursing.

In 1853 the Crimean War broke out. It was the latest bloody event in a long drawn-out struggle between the great powers of Europe over influence in the crumbling Ottoman empire. The war became notorious for the terrible conditions of the wounded and the great logistical incompetency. A violent storm destroyed almost thirty ships. Medicine, food and clothes sank to the bottom of the sea. Cholera ravaged the troops and at home in Great Britain people were shocked. This was the first modern war, not just in the sense that it used trenches and blind artillery fire, but also because the telegraph made it possible to quickly send messages across long distances. With that it became the first war that the media could monitor in real time. The newspapers reported home on the misery and, like many others, Florence Nightingale felt compelled to do something. On 21 October 1854 she travelled with thirty-eight volunteer nurses to the Black Sea. The field hospital lay on a mountain in Skutari outside Istanbul, and already before the ship arrived an article had appeared in the British press about the remarkable leader of the expedition. Who was this Miss Nightingale? Women in military medical services – it caused a sensation.

In the sick house in Skutari in the Asian part of Constantinople, the personnel were overworked, the standard of hygiene was awful, mass infections wrought havoc and people were left on the dirty floors to die. With her own money and funds that the readers of *The Times* newspaper had collected, Florence Nightingale started to buy what was needed. She rented a house near the field hospital and started a laundry. Produce was bought at local markets and she made sure the soldiers were fed citrus fruits. A diet without fruit led to diseases associated with malnutrition, she realized. Previously, the food had mostly consisted of raw meat that was handed out in portions. Often rotten. Now she employed a star chef from London.

The sanitization work that began dramatically reduced mortality rates, and Nightingale kept meticulous statistics of the successes. Consistently opposed by military doctors, she revolutionized nursing. When she returned to London, she was a national hero. Not at all the social scandal her family had expected. On the contrary, Florence Nightingale became a legend. She was depicted as a fair lady in a white uniform watching over sick rooms full of the wounded. They called her 'the Lady with the Lamp', and the media delightedly repeated this epithet. A guiding star of kindness, mildness and duty during dark hospital nights.

Florence Nightingale's image is still that of a quiet, shy, discreet angel disinterested in money. In reality she was a pugnacious social critic with a great interest in economics. Statistics were her weapon in the fight for a new way of thinking about nursing. Not the blushing, self-denying altruism that she has been attributed with since.

God and mammon aren't enemies, Florence Nightingale suggested. Just because it's God's work that's being carried out doesn't mean that nurses shouldn't get paid. The thought that there is no contradiction between doing good deeds and striving for prosperity comes up again and again in her writings. Money is a necessary means for those who want to do God's work here on earth.

Florence Nightingale fought her entire life for good wages in nursing. This we've chosen to forget. We are stuck in the idea that you do something either for money or out of empathy, and this notion is closely linked to our picture of the sexes. Men are driven by self-interest and women are supposed to make the whole picture come together.

We are not encouraged to imagine that both driving forces can be found in one and the same person, irrespective of sex. Even if that's what's closest to the truth.

Just as our impetus to pick the children up on time from

day care or to let the authorities put a nuclear waste facility in our backyard is more complex than only being about crass calculations and economic gain, so too is the motivation to pursue care work. It's not about how women are born to break their backs and souls in the service of humanity or to give society a soft counterbalance to the hard market.

Not even Florence Nightingale, the very symbol of self-sacrificing care work, was a 'Florence Nightingale'. But the myth of care as an inexhaustible natural resource that we can reap from feminine nature is unshakeable. Because we need it to be.

We made Florence Nightingale what we wanted her to be. Exactly what man needed so his society could fit together.

The question is whether it's a sustainable long-term strategy.

Today there is a shortage of care workers in the world. The time when a large group of women didn't have the opportunity to work in any other sector has passed. At least in the West.

Around 3,500 Filipino doctors were retrained as nurses between 2000 and 2003. Most of them migrated to the United States. A nurse there earns four to six times more than a doctor in the Philippines.

Educated nurses migrate from countries across the African continent to South Africa. And from there to Canada and from Canada to the USA. Sub-Saharan African countries suffer from 24% of all the illnesses in the world, but only have 3% of the world's nursing personnel. In Zambia there are 2.2 nurses per 10,000 people. That's more than forty times less than in the United States.

In this market one goes where the money is.

Women want to build better lives for themselves, and many countries are drained of care workers. Even in the West, our problem isn't solved. In Sweden there is expected to be a deficit of 130,000 qualified care workers in 2030. The same year, the USA will suffer from a shortage of between 400,000 and 800,000 qualified nurses.

Even if nursing wages in rich western countries are high compared with what people earn in other parts of the world, they are low compared with the rest of the job market. That makes it difficult to recruit. Money seems to matter.

Does this make care work less noble? Less important?

For economic man it doesn't matter whether something is about money or not. He is still selfish. Whether it's about his salary, if he should kill himself, or which way he should drive to work. Real people, on the other hand, carry their complex motives and driving forces with them – even in their relationship to money.

Researchers have studied money in relation to the desire to do good. Care, ethics, loyalty and taking pleasure in doing a job can very well disappear if you add money in as a motive. It's not as simple as the more motives we have, the more willing we are to do a job well – as with the day care pick-up in Israel or the Swiss referendum on the nuclear waste facility.

However, the studies found that if money was seen as the acknowledgement of work, our own motives are strengthened. Then it makes us more happy and motivated.

People want to feel appreciated and supported in their jobs, and money is one way to show this. Above all, people need money. Even women. No one wants to feel exploited, and just because something is about money, that doesn't mean that it is selfish.

Adam Smith wanted to conserve love in a jar. On the label, economists wrote 'women'. The contents weren't allowed to be mixed with anything else and had to be kept locked away. This 'other economy' was seen as something entirely separate. Without importance for the whole, and actually it wasn't an economy at all, but an inexhaustible natural resource.

Later the Chicago economists concluded that this other economy wasn't just irrelevant to explaining how prosperity was created, it simply didn't exist. It was just as good to run our families and our marriages using the rules of the market.

Nothing else existed.

If we really had wanted to conserve love and care in society, instead of excluding it we should have tried to support it with money and resources. We should have organized the economy around what was important for people. But we did the opposite.

We redefined people to fit our idea of the economy.

CHAPTER ELEVEN

In which we see that a negative number is still zero

In 1978 Deng Xiaoping began to liberalize the Chinese economy. Chairman Mao had died two years before and a wave of increased prosperity swept over Japan, Taiwan, Hong Kong and South Korea. Market principles, not central planning.

China's interests had to be protected.

The Communist Party declared that economic growth was 'the central task' and in two decades China was transformed from a walled garden into a capitalist phenomenon. Never before has the world seen such growth. From the dominance of the proletariat to that of the economist, they were everywhere: writing privatization plans, taking over companies they had just privatized, pushing aside the old Maoists.

Deng Xiaoping was met with resistance from within the party. Reforms were implemented gradually. It wasn't the shock therapy Russia had known. They were cautious, taking one step at a time. No one talked about the end game – but it was clear who was in charge. Economists became the new high priests of Chinese civilization – educated in western economic theories yet loyal to the Chinese project. The ideas of neoliberal economists were packaged in quotes from Karl Marx and Chairman Mao.

Shanghai today is being built up so quickly that the city map has to be redrawn every other week. Three hundred million people have gone from agrarian life to modernity in thirty years, a process that took over two centuries in the West. The middle class is growing at record speed. The highest number of female self-made billionaires is in China. Cheung Yan, who chairs one of Asia's largest paper producers, is worth more than twice as much as Oprah Winfrey.

Meanwhile, acid rain falls over a third of China's land. Grey-brown mist. Four hundred thousand premature deaths related to sulphur each year. Environmental suicide.

The protests in Tiananmen Square in 1989 were primarily about a demand for democracy and freedom of speech. The discontent with the neoliberal reforms that had caused inequality and inflation the year before were also a part of it. And when Deng Xiaoping early in the morning of the fourth of June ordered the massacre of the demonstrators, it wasn't just the call for democracy in China that was silenced. As the tanks stormed the square, the public debate about equality died. At least for the next fifteen years.

Chinese workers have earned less and less in proportion to the country's GDP each year since 1983, and the working conditions in factories are terrible. When fourteen employees in a sixteen-month period killed themselves at iPhone manufacturer Foxconn, salaries were raised by 30%. At the same time, workers had to sign a contract that they wouldn't commit suicide. If they did, their families would receive the least possible amount of compensation.

But suicide isn't the only problem. *Guolaosi* means 'death from being overworked' in Mandarin.

It is so common they have a word for it.

Months after Deng Xiaoping's first reforms, Paul Volcker took over as Chairman of the Federal Reserve. It was July 1979 and inflation in America was so high that it had become a self-fulfilling prophecy. Everyone expected each dollar to be worth less tomorrow than it was worth today. To compensate, wages and prices were increased, which in turn made the dollar worth less and less, whereby salaries and prices were raised even more.

Paul Volcker decided that inflation should be combatted. Cost what it may. Within a few months, he reconfigured America's monetary policy. When Ronald Reagan became president of the United States two years later, unemployment was at 8.4% and inflation was still in double digits. Reagan tried on the one hand to stimulate the economy with large tax cuts and high military expenditure while also calling for the Federal Reserve to put the brakes on the economy with higher interest rates and a monetary policy designed to increase the cost of borrowing.

Margaret Thatcher was already prime minister in Great Britain. The trade union movement would be reined in, the government would shrink and the former British Empire's economy would be restarted. They found each other, Thatcher and Reagan.

It was a new era.

Neoliberalism, a previously obscure political doctrine, was brought in and put at the centre of the projects of her and Reagan. 'There is no such thing as society,' said Thatcher. All that existed were free individuals and their families. No community or collectivity.

In its purest form, neoliberalism wants to reduce the role of the State to printing money and organizing the military, the police and the justice system. The role of politics would be to maintain a distinct framework of privatization, free markets and free trade. Beyond that, nothing. Except in the areas where there aren't markets: land, water, care, pollution, education. There, the State must intervene and actively create markets. Privatize, tear up and create market-like relationships. Everything should be able to be bought and sold. Only then will human society work.

In the neoliberal theories, politics should create and maintain competition. Let the wheels spin and the pie get bigger.

Neoliberalism's poets, such as the philosopher Friedrich Hayek or the economist Milton Friedman, were often more nuanced in their rhetoric than the politicians who followed in their footsteps, but the basic thought was the same: lower taxes, smaller government and less regulation in the financial sector.

If you let the individual be, in the job market as in the stock market, then the economy will grow. Economic man will work, start companies, do business and maximize his gains. It is in his very nature to do so, so don't bother him. Don't diminish his drive to strive. Large welfare programmes only destroy the market. Security sedates people. Why, then, would people work?

Economic man always does what is most rational, and if he gets money from the State for being unemployed or sick, then he'll be unemployed or sick – because he benefits from it.

The world's resources are limited, and this leads to discipline because people are forced to compete with each other to survive. Market solutions and large gaps in society are therefore one way to keep people in order. If people got what they needed without being forced to compete for it, then there wouldn't be a reason for them to be disciplined.

Therefore, it is immoral to give people things according to their need rather than pushing them to work for it. It is an incentive for people to be less than what they can be, and that does them a disservice. We are all rational, and if we build a system where it is rational to be lazy – then that's the society we'll get.

The conclusion of this perspective is that there will always be winners and losers. Those in society who are more disciplined will win, and therefore they deserve their success. Earning money becomes a sign that one is a good person. That's why it's reasonable to lower taxes for high-income earners.

Lack of success, in turn, is a sign of lack of discipline. That's why it is only right that the less disciplined should serve the more disciplined. There will be plenty of work for them to do in the large, poorly paid service sector that develops. Let one and all work to their greatest ability and let the free market both inspire and chasten us to diligence and prosperity.

The rhetoric of Margaret Thatcher and Ronald Reagan was in this way about curing seriously ailing economies with simple principles. But neither Thatcher nor Reagan succeeded in getting their respective countries to perform in the way they promised during the 1980s. After the depression at the start of the decade, the American and British economies started to grow (which economies usually do when a depression starts to turn), inflation was combatted and interest rates fell, but unemployment was sky high. Both Great Britain and the USA saw growing chasms and a very slow increase in productivity during this period.

Neoliberal ideas may have dominated the debate during the eighties, but economically West Germany and Japan were the success stories of that decade. Countries that indeed had inflation-fighting central banks, but that hadn't swallowed the neoliberal reform package.

West Germany had high wages and strong unions, the Japanese economy was characterized by large investments from the State. In spite of this, everyone was seduced by neo-liberalism.

It was so much more than an economic programme.

Neoliberalism's economic theories arrived on the scene and promised to slay stagflation, the two-headed monster that had appeared in the global economy at the end of the 1970s. High inflation *and* high unemployment. Both nuisances at once. This was supposed to be impossible.

Mainstream economists influenced by John Maynard Keynes were convinced that if unemployment decreased, inflation would increase. And vice versa. When almost all workers were employed, they'd have the negotiation power to increase their wages and then prices would also rise. When unemployment increased, the opposite should occur. It was simply one or the other. Stagflation showed that it wasn't really this simple and when old assumptions are questioned, new, untested ones can come into play. But no one could have imagined just how untested these new theories were.

'To help the poor and middle classes,' wrote the American author George Gilder, 'one must cut the tax rates of the rich.' His book *Wealth and Poverty* was published in 1981 and sold over one million copies. Ronald Reagan enthusiastically handed it out to friends and advisers. Comprising a moral theory of capitalism's infallibility, the ideas that Gilder presented were irresistible: if the richest could only grow richer, this would serve the economy as a whole.

To lower taxes for the rich is the best thing we can do for the poor: if the rich have more money in their wallets, they'll start companies, invest in new technologies and with that contribute to growth, Gilder asserted. There would be more jobs, and people who previously were unemployed would start working in the companies that the rich were starting. They'd earn a salary and pay tax on that salary. Then even the State's revenue would increase.

The State, then, gets back the money it had lost by lowering taxes. One minus one is no longer zero.

It was witchcraft and too good to be true. Even George Bush Senior called these theories 'Voodoo economics'.

Which of course they were.

In 1974 economist Arthur Laffer, *Wall Street Journal* writer Jude Wanniski and one Dick Cheney met in a hotel room in Washington, DC. The would-be American vice-president

Cheney is said to at first have had difficulty understanding the theory the others were discussing. But Arthur Laffer pulled out a napkin and drew a curve.

The premise for the curve was simple: if the State decides that tax is zero per cent, then the State will get zero dollars in tax revenue. If the State decides that taxes are 100%, then the States will also get zero dollars in tax revenue. It will no longer be worth it to work. So no one will and the State won't get any tax revenue.

Because no one is working.

Between these two points, Laffer drew a curve. It seemed to depict that a radical decrease in taxation, against all logic, could give the State more – not less – income. At some point, Cheney's eyes grew wide: you can dramatically lower taxes without creating a deficit in the State's finances?

Jude Wanniski eventually wrote a book with the tender title *The Way The World Works*. Along with George Gilder's *Wealth and Poverty*, it was the book that spread Laffer's idea among the western world's elite.

There seemed to be no limits to what the simple Laffer curve could explain. It was so simple and yet at the same time our whole existence seemed to revolve around it. According to Wanniski, even a baby in the crib understood Laffer's basic theories.

Infants who can't even walk yet, he wrote, learn 'something that politicians and economists frequently forget, which is that there are always two rates of taxation that produce the same revenue.'

The child finds that if he lays quietly in his crib, his mother will stay in the room next door. The 'tax rate' on the mother is zero and the infant's 'revenue' in terms of attentiveness is zero. Conversely, if the infant is always crying and demanding attention he will soon discover that even in this case the mother will stop coming in to comfort him. The 'tax rate' is, in other words, 100% and the 'revenue' is again zero.

From these fantasies about child rearing and the infant's inner rational life, surprising conclusions can be drawn, according to Wanniski. Even if one lowers taxes by 200 billion dollars, budget deficits will not explode. But of course they did. One hundred billion. Then 200 billion.

David Stockman, Reagan's director of the Office of Management and Budget, wrote: 'By 1982, I knew the Reagan Revolution was impossible.'

In other words, Laffer's theory didn't succeed in negating the fundamental fact that one minus one is still zero.

Now matter how much Reagan wanted to lower taxation on the rich.

These years, which did not improve the economy as a whole, were the start of one of the largest redistributions in world history. From the many to the few.

The richest 0.1% of America's population tripled its share of the national revenue between 1978 and 1999. In Great Britain the richest percentile doubled its share during the same period: from 6.5% in 1982 to 13% in 2005. And in Russia, after the neoliberal shock therapy, a super-rich elite quickly pulled away from the rest of society. Today Moscow has more billionaires than any other city in the world.

In 1970, a CEO in the USA earned thirty times as much as an average worker. At the turn of the millennium, this number was up to 500. In his day, the famous financier J. P. Morgan thought that the average head of an American company didn't need to earn more than twenty times that of an employee. By 2007, this had increased to 364 times. And American standards drove up the salaries of CEOs across the western world. In the UK executive pay trebled between 2002 and 2012. The ratio of the total rewards of chief executive officers of FTSE 100 companies rose from 45 times the pay of the average employee in 1998 to 120 times in 2010.

Today, the world's dollar-billionaires, just over 1,000 people, have a total fortune that is greater than that of the poorest 2.5 billion people. In the USA, more of the total income increase between 1979 and 2007 has gone to the richest 1% than to the bottom 90%.

Seldom have so few gotten so much.

That the highest earners have pulled away so rapidly has a lot to do with globalization. J. K. Rowling, who wrote the Harry Potter books, earns an enormous amount more than Charles Dickens did in his time because the book market is global. But this mechanism can't explain the gaps in development in all sectors.

According to the UN, the world in 2005 was less equal than it was ten years before, in spite of the economic progress of many regions. The richest countries are now on average more than 100 times richer than the poorest. One hundred years ago, the ratio was more like nine to one.

The super-rich are growing ever more powerful, and among the world's super-rich are still very few women. In an age where women increasingly hold important posts in companies, it's notable that only fifteen female heads of companies are found on the Fortune 500 list. The Sunday Times Rich List, an annual round-up of the 1,000 wealthiest people in Britain, consisted of only 7% women in 2007. By 2011 the number had increased to 11%. On a similar German ranking of multi-million-euro plutocrats, only one in six was female. The super-rich women of the world have mainly inherited their wealth, not made it. There are only fourteen female billionaires who have earned their own fortune and, including them, women still only make up 9% of dollar-billionaires in the world. This pattern of female wealth equalling inherited wealth is so prominent that Lena Edlund and Wojciech Kopczuk of Columbia University have been able to show that the more wealth that is held by women, the more stagnant the economy is.

This doesn't mean that rich women slow down growth.

Only that when growth is slow the main way to get rich is to inherit money.

And inherit money is what women do.

As daughters, wives and widows.

In the 1980s, something called 'paper entrepreneurship' arose. In step with the deregulation of the financial sector, many of the most talented people in the western world started devoting themselves to finding new ways of trading with paper – even though our need for innovation in society was hardly most pressing in this sector.

Still, that's where the money was.

In 2008, 41% of Harvard Business School graduates went on to work with hedge funds, investment banks and capital risk companies. This was a new record. The same autumn, Lehman Brothers filed for bankruptcy, and the financial crisis became a reality. The value of fifty billion dollars was destroyed in eighteen months, fifty-three million people were pushed into poverty.

For speculation on the financial market to career so wildly out of control that it topples the whole economy, there have to be people with so much money that they are immune to risk. When all the money is collected at the top of a society, people invest their fortunes in assets that seem most likely to attract other large investors. This leads to prices on certain stocks or properties simply growing and growing. These types of speculative bubbles always burst sooner or later. Extreme inequality and financial crisis usually coincide. But the elite who cause it usually come out OK. And usually they are men.

For every crisis that the financial sector has created, it has earned more and more money.

During the era that preceded the crisis of the 1930s, the division of wealth in the USA was almost identical to what it was before the financial crisis of 2008. One per cent earned 24% of the USA's total income. In 1928 as in 2008. And when the money moves upwards, so too does political power.

The rich and powerful can of course impact the shape and application of the rules of the global economy to a greater degree than anyone else. This also applies to the rules that are meant to restrict them.

'God is with everybody ... and in the long run, he plumps for the people who have the most money and the biggest armies,' wrote the French dramatist Jean Anouilh.

Economic man is the hero of this world. He's simultaneously its aspiration and its legitimation. He is the story through which it makes sense of itself and preaches its message: if the rich grow richer, it will help us all. God help us all.

Economic man is the one who tells us that nothing else is possible, and as long as we keep trying to be like him nothing else ever will be possible.

CHAPTER TWELVE

In which we all become entrepreneurs

The world's tallest building is in Dubai. The country is one of the seven self-governing emirates that make up the United Arab Emirates. Record growth, no democracy, no political parties, no income tax and no trade unions.

A neoliberal theme park in the middle of the desert.

The society has been called Milton Friedman's beach club after the renowned right-wing economist. For many years, Dubai had the highest growth rate in the world and was held up as a utopia of freedom. Most things were deregulated, and the economy gained momentum. At one point it was estimated that 15% of all construction cranes in the world were in the little emirate. The country's unofficial bank holiday is an annual shopping festival that attracts everyone from the Beckham family to Afghan drug lords. But around the city are the camps where the guest workers live.

Six to twelve people in each room, often without a kitchen or toilet.

They built the city, but they are invisible to its inhabitants. As invisible as the thousands of Russian, Indian, Iranian and Armenian prostitutes whose bodies are sold at luxury hotels by the mafia. All to attract foreign investors. The freedom that Dubai is famous for was to a large degree the freedom men had to buy women's bodies.

Politics exists to give the market what it needs. Cheap labour, space to play, sex, entertainment and subsidies. The crown prince of Dubai has been referred to as the CEO of Dubai, Ltd. He governs the emirate like a company in the service of private industries.

The dream of a neoliberal utopia has probably never been taken further than this.

A luxury world far out in the sand constructed so it can deny the inequality and environmental devastation that it itself produces.

According to the American feminist Wendy Brown, the neoliberal ideology does not in fact truly conceive of the market as something 'natural'; instead, neoliberalism tries to manufacture the reality that it insists already exists.

On the one hand, it is assumed that people are first and foremost competitive. On the other hand, the incentives for individuals to compete must be continuously increased using political means: deregulation, lowering taxes and clearance sales.

On the one hand it is assumed that all people everywhere are interested in growing rich. On the other hand, taxes have to be lowered so that it pays to be rich.

Competition is said to be the foundation of all social relations, while it is precisely these competitive relationships that have to be encouraged and created through politics. It's not a natural state of affairs, but rather one that must be constructed and maintained. Neoliberals don't want to do away with politics, they just want different politics, that's what the crown prince of Dubai understood.

Economic man needs some help getting going, and so neoliberalism develops institutions, incentives and methods to support the vision of the completely competition-focused, rational individual. The purpose is to incite market-oriented decision-making on all fronts.

People aren't focused on gain and competition in every aspect of their lives. But it's the task of neoliberalism to spread and institutionalize this kind of desire. Through privatization and through governing everything from education to environmental politics, nursing and care using the same market principles as for tomatoes, that's how we'll create this kind of world – where only one kind of logic is allowed. Using political means, one must create markets where there weren't markets before and then use all available political means to maintain them.

Neoliberalism is not at all the same thing as laissez-faire, the economic school that thinks that if we just let things be the economy will blossom.

Contemporary laissez-faire economics is the most extreme embodiment of the idea Adam Smith expressed in the metaphor of the invisible hand. Smith himself didn't advocate this kind of politics – perhaps better described as the near complete lack thereof – but there are those who interpret his ideas in this way. They should not, however, be confused with neoliberals.

Neoliberalism doesn't want to do away with politics – neoliberalism wants to put politics at the service of the market. Neoliberals don't think that the economy should be left in peace, but rather they are for the economy being guided, supported and protected through the spreading of social norms that facilitate competition and rational behaviour.

Neoliberal economic theory isn't built on keeping the hands of politics off the market, it's built on keeping the hands of politics busy with satisfying the needs of the market.

It's not true that neoliberalism doesn't want to pursue monetary, fiscal, family or criminal policies. It is rather that monetary, fiscal, family and criminal policies should all be used to procure what the market needs.

The French philosopher Michel Foucault thought that liberalism and neoliberalism distinguished themselves from each other in how they perceived economic activity. Classical liberalism was focused on exchange: Adam Smith wrote about how people bought and traded. The idea that you give in order to get something in return was seen as the cornerstone of our society. What have you given and what have you got back? Was it fair? Was it handled correctly?

Existence was seen as the sum of and consequence of a number of exchanges, transactions and contracts. Liberalism took the market's logic of exchange and decided to view the world through this lens. Politics was seen as a series of contracts: citizens exchanged certain freedoms for the guarantee of security from the State. What have you given and what have you got back? Was it fair? Was it handled correctly?

Even other relationships were interpreted using this logic.

Neoliberalism, however, doesn't put its emphasis on exchange but focuses instead on competition. Competition is the grounding idea through which the world is interpreted.

If people don't compete, then they can't function. More than a specific idea about the role of the State or monetary policy, this is the foundation for the neoliberal ideology, according to Foucault. And whereas liberals and Adam Smith saw exchange as something natural, neoliberals see competition as a relationship that has to be constructed.

Competition is the most fundamental part of society, but at the same time it is an artificial relationship. It has to be protected, partly against the market's tendency to create monopolies, partly against the meddlesome fingers of politics. It presupposes constant State intervention, not in the market itself, but in the conditions for the market. That is, in people. Because our existence is the market's fundamental condition of being.

'Economics are the method; the object is to change the heart and soul,' said Margaret Thatcher.

Classical liberalism differentiates between people as citizens and people as economic subjects. That's not so in neoliberalism. There is only one relationship, and that is economic. In other words, there is no reason to differentiate the citizen from the worker from the consumer. It's one and the same person. Economic man. Nice to meet you.

More than a political programme, neoliberalism is a new interpretation of what it means to be a person.

For Karl Marx, the development of capital was a process through which workers' knowledge, skill and humanity was mechanized bit by bit. In the morning, the worker went to a factory he didn't own to make products that he didn't have any say over that someone else would buy so the factory owner could earn more money.

The worker produced things for someone else, for other people to buy with the help of his own body. He – for it was always a man – was turned bit by bit into a cog, part of something that wasn't his own. Something interchangeable and less human.

Something that only has its chains to lose.

Karl Marx tells the story with three characters. The Worker is the labour, the Machine he is bent over is fixed capital and the Money that his work generates is fluid capital. The conflict between work and capital is the intrigue that everything revolves around and that (literally) drives history forward. These are the classic characters within economics, whether one wants to tell Marxist stories with them or whether one prefers other stories.

At the end of the 1950s, American economists thought they had discovered something new. But it was actually something that economists had come up with long ago but had forgotten.

In *The Wealth of Nations*, Adam Smith mentions a concept he calls 'human capital'. People's education, skills, talents and competencies can, according to Smith, be seen as a form of capital. If you as a factory owner invest in your workers' abilities and knowledge, it can have the same effect as investing in a new machine.

You send your employees on a course to learn a new technology and, hey presto, they can produce twice as much. You're making an investment. The course cost money, and additionally, it cost you to shut down production for a whole afternoon, but eventually you earn it all back and you even make a profit. People's abilities can, in other words, be seen as a form of capital. It's possible to make more or less successful investments in them and they can grow.

The Chicago economists found the term 'human capital' in Smith and included it in their theories. How the term has changed the economy of the modern job market and whether it is good or bad is a different conversation. What Foucault meant was that when the term 'human capital' is used widely, as the neoliberals have used it, it does something to the economic view of people.

And this 'something' has a significance that reaches far beyond economic science.

'It may seem odd now, but I hesitated a while before deciding to call my book *Human Capital*,' said Chicago economist Gary Becker in his Nobel lecture in 1992. Today the book is considered a classic. 'In the early days many people were criticizing this term and the underlying analysis because they believed that it treated people like slaves or machines. My, how things have changed!'

And indeed they have. Through the term 'human capital', every person has been transformed into an entrepreneur in the business of selling themselves. Today we more or less take this concept for granted.

If you educate yourself, you invest in yourself, and you can therefore expect a greater return in the future. If you choose to migrate to another country, it's also an investment in your human capital. A rational calculation of future returns. If you quit school you're refraining from investment. And in turn, the return will be less. The salary you earn isn't a salary any more, but rather a return on capital. Your life is your small business and the capital is, in this case, you.

*

Foucault thought that with the concept of human capital, economic man stopped being a person who buys and sells on a market. Instead he became an entrepreneur of himself. He became, critics said, a machine.

There are no workers in neoliberal history. There are only people who invest in their human capital. Entrepreneurs whose own lives are business projects and who bear full, sole responsibility for the outcome. If you succeed, you've invested well, if you fail, you've invested poorly.

And so, economics became something other than one form of logic among many. It became a way of life. A person wanders around, makes decisions, lives her life, educates herself or neglects to educate herself and the effects of this are accumulated in her human capital.

Economic man is no longer a person who trades things with others, as Adam Smith had imagined people to be. Economic man is an apparatus who invests in himself. If you rob a bank, quit medical school, whiten your teeth – everything is a choice, made like any other business decision, by calculating future gains and losses. More or less successful investments in yourself. The economic system becomes synonymous with human nature, and you can't question your deepest essence.

The conflict Marx spoke of dissolves, but not in the way he imagined. It's not the means of production that have changed – instead, the meaning of being human has changed.

Neoliberalism resolves conflicts between work and capital by simply turning a person into capital – and her life into a series of investments she makes in her market value. Christian theologians suggested that one could feed a whole congregation with a crust of bread and one fish. We believe that you can feed yourself. We believe in you. It may be a hard world – but it breathes for you. There is no alternative. And the universe genuflects.

It's a viewpoint that has made us all equal. The woman at the unemployment agency and the man who waits for his fake documents outside the airport in Dhaka. Each is equally a self-entrepreneur. Just like the CEO who stretches his legs out in his aeroplane seat to catch a few hours' sleep before his next meeting on the other side of eight hours in business class. No difference between them, just better or worse investments in the capital that is you. And in the amount of start-up capital that you were born with. But what else can be applied to growth? My breast enhancement was an investment, the soap opera star says smoothly. Peel away layer after layer and it's economics all the way. Your life translated into a series of investments you make in your own value.

If you take this point of view seriously – and there is no point of view taken more seriously – then you have fundamentally changed what it means to be human.

CHAPTER THIRTEEN

In which we see that the uterus isn't a space capsule

In 1965 Swedish photographer Lennart Nilsson published his groundbreaking keyhole pictures of foetuses. First in *LIFE* magazine and then in the book *A Child Is Born*.

Nilsson had experimented with electron microscopes since 1953, and the book project had taken him almost twelve years. The 30 April 1965 issue of *LIFE* magazine took the whole world by surprise and sold eight million copies in the first four days alone.

Crouched, with a large head and fin-like arms, the foetus floats freely inside a balloon of water. This is how we've become accustomed to picturing the beginning of our own existences. The baby floats, an independent astronaut, with only an umbilical cord connecting it to the world around. The mother doesn't exist. She has become a void – the already autonomous tiny space hero flies forth. The womb is just a room.

But no one can separate themselves from the place where the gaze originates. The camera's lens is said to be objective. But Lennart Nilsson's photographs are a depiction – not an accurate representation of the world. What we see in extreme magnification and in dramatically cropped photos isn't reality.

Existence in the belly isn't free-floating and desolate. Few things could be further from the truth. The foetus grows out of the mother, in the mother and in constant contact with the mother. It's cramped, throbbing, pulsing and you can't really tell where the mother ends and the foetus begins.

In Lennart Nilsson's pictures, this dependency isn't visible. The foetus is alone. The mother is eradicated. The pictures don't show any relationship between mother and child: we are born complete, self-sufficient individuals.

The picture of life, as depicted by Lennart Nilsson, dropped into our collective imagination and there it stayed. We must have found it rather appealing.

The question is why.

We have been taught that our societies are built on rational contracts and our economies on free markets. That manufacturers and consumers, employers and employees – everything – are one and the same consciousness in different forms. Different expressions of one and the same reasoning. The world, the impersonal sum of the individual's free choices.

Actually, society is more like a form of war. It's exploitative, racist and patriarchal. The economic reality is more 'the survival of the fittest', the rich grow richer and the rest of us chase after them. On some level, we know this. But still we continue to fantasize.

For centuries we have been fed stories about how society arose because people made a rational decision to unite. After establishing that we would all benefit from a collaborative structure, we started to depend on each other. No sooner, no later.

This creation myth is told in countless variations, and like most other myths, it's a mind game. It's hard to imagine it really happened this way: there we were sat hunched over in our caves. Darkness, cold, other squatting figures in other caves, impossible to determine who was friend, foe, human or mammoth. Suddenly, one person stands and exclaims:

– Hey, listen up! Why don't we join forces and help each other as part of a society? We can trade things with each other, everyone will benefit from that!

Hardly.

But that's our fantasy of self-sufficiency. And it's seductive.

Lennart Nilsson's famous photographs are variations on the same theme. On the cover of *LIFE* magazine, a small person floats alone in what looks like a transparent space capsule. It's an existence in the womb that is completely independent of the womb. The foetus is a free individual, and the woman's body doesn't exist. The mother is a space that the foetus is renting. In comes sperm, out goes baby. Pregnancy is a woman in a rocking chair by a window for nine months. That's your mother. She is a passive storage unit. You were inside her, but you were independent from the start. Master of the empty space you floated in.

The foetus in Lennart Nilsson's pictures sucks on its thumb and stares into the darkness behind closed eyes. Around him everything is black and the placenta is a space station floating free in the distance. This is a creation myth about free individuals that was fitting for its time. It's 1965 when the pictures are published. Lyndon B. Johnson is president and the USA has increased its presence in Vietnam. In London,

Winston Churchill has passed away and the word 'fuck' is spoken for the first time on British television. In Nilsson's homeland, IKEA opens its second warehouse and the Rolling Stones play their first gig in the country at Stockholm's Kungliga Tennishallen.

In most of the pictures, Lennart Nilsson was actually photographing dead embryos. It gave him the chance to play with light, background and composition. They were fantastic photographs. But what had been composed to depict life, was in fact its absence.

For more than thirty years we've known that the assumptions about people in the standard economic models aren't right. Economic man doesn't exist – at least not in reality. But we still cling to him. However much he is criticized, he is still synonymous with economics, and we allow him to take up more and more space in our lives.

It doesn't seem to matter what the research says. It doesn't seem to matter how often the economic models we build contribute to crashing the global economy. It doesn't seem to matter how they time and time again fail to predict a swell in the market, its panic attacks and whims. We still won't let go.

We scrape up bits of an imagined universe, put them together in models and call it an accurate-enough picture of the world.

The suppositions around economic man have time and time again been shown not to hold. But even though Kahneman and Tversky could show that our decisions weren't at all objective and rational over thirty years ago, it didn't change much. That we know economic man doesn't really exist doesn't seem to stop us from putting him at the centre of economic science and from applying his logic to ever greater portions of our lives. In 2004 the international phenomenon *Freakonomics* declared that every part of our existence conformed to the principles of the market. At the end of the seventies the French left-wing philosopher Michel Foucault couldn't imagine that even the wildest neoliberals would take their theories that far. Yet there it is, a bestselling paperback in the centre aisle.

There have always been economists who have vocally and meticulously criticized economic man. But he is, in spite of it all, still synonymous with economics. It's him we refer to when we talk about 'economic logic' in our daily lives, and the schools of criticism that have emerged in opposition to him are treated, in the best cases, as complementary. It's economic man who occupies the centre, and it's to him that everyone else must relate.

Behavioural economics, the school that has made the biggest impact in recent years, has gone to great pains to show that people don't always only care about their own profits, that justice matters and that preferences can change over time.

Behavioural economics has shown that people don't always handle information correctly and that we don't always make decisions that are in line with our preferences. All this is very important and a big step forward in relation to the theories that provide economic man's foundation. At the same time, economic man is still the starting point for behavioural economics. Through experiments and studies, behavioural economists try to document exceptions to the rule, but the lone individual is still both the ideal and the premise. Behavioural economics reasons that because it's clearly difficult for people to act rationally, we need to be helped along. We need support, and we need to be pushed in the right direction. We are quite simply not perfect economic agents. The role of the State is therefore to create better incentives, and with its help, to encourage us to act more in line with our preferences.

Politically this often results in measures being focused on getting people to, for example, use less electricity by giving them better information, which will make it easier for them to make rational decisions. Not by raising the carbon tax or by the State investing in green technology and energy-efficient cities. Similarly, obesity should be combatted by making it easier to find information about the sugar content of various products. Not by actually getting a handle on the problems within the food and grocery industry.

Of course, it's not behavioural economists' fault that their analysis is used to create shortcuts for politicians who want to avoid making difficult decisions. The theories are certainly a step in the right direction. But they don't change the fact that economics is still a science of choice – not a science about how society will survive, keep house and evolve. No overview of society and how people are created and formed in relation to each other is found within behavioural economics. Economics remains the study of the individual. It asserts that dependency is not a natural part of being human, and power relationships aren't economically relevant.

Economic man, in other words, hasn't budged.

'We are all human,' we often say when we want to point to a shared commonality. Something that unites us beyond class, gender, race, age, background and experience. As though humanity were created outside class, gender, race, age, background and experience – rather than *through* class, gender, race, age, background and experience. Instead we see circumstances, the body and context as layers that have to be peeled away. They cloud the vision. If we want to talk about how things really are, we must abstract how things really are, we think.

But being human is experienced precisely through a gender, a body, a social position, and the backgrounds and experiences that we have. There is no other way.

But we suppose that it's precisely this that we must deny. That we must find a rational consciousness that is the same for each of us.

'Women are individuals, too,' we say. To be an individual has become synonymous with being human and the individual is the elementary particle of economics.

Economic man, however, is a very specific idea about what it means to be human. Economics became 'the science of the individual' and the word 'individual' means, precisely, indivisible. The smallest part that the whole can be divided into. Like the atom in Newton's physics. If you understood the individual, you understood everything. The individual is, however, not the same thing as a person.

Half of humanity's most significant distinguishing feature is precisely that it is divisible.

All women can't give birth. All women don't want to give birth. But what differentiates the female body from the male body is that it can become pregnant and give birth. That which was one person can divide itself and become two. This is how all people have come into being. We are born from each other. And we live from each other, in each other and through each other.

We don't start our lives in a state of independence and then face the challenge of creating some sort of relationship or bond with others. But when we are supposed to argue for the importance of a society we almost always start here: with an autonomous individual, and then we enumerate the reasons why he should create dependencies and relationships.

– It'll be easier to produce food.

– It'll be easier to defend ourselves against wild animals.

– It will make him happier.

– He can get help when he is sick.

– He will live longer.

There are many advantages to having other people around. As if we had ever had any other choice.

The process is actually the opposite. We are born into other people's demands and expectations. To be a child is to be almost completely dependent on others. We have never known anything else. Totally at the mercy of their hopes, demands, love, neuroses, traumas, disappointments and unrealized lives. To take care of a child is in a way to constantly be meeting the needs of another, and from this intimacy, the child must learn, step by step, to become more independent. As the feminist theorist Virginia Held has pointed out: the natural human state is to be enveloped by our dependency on others. The challenge is to break out of this and find one's own identity. Carve out more and more space for one's self. From within a context of other people, relationships and the world they bring, you set out to find what's you.

Those who take care of the child must themselves be able to support a separate identity. Not be swallowed by constant engagement or to be enticed into finding all of their value by being so completely needed by someone else. Managing to do this and to keep the relationships of mutual dependency healthy is the challenge that shapes most lives and societies. Every day and every hour. So many of the mental and emotional wounds that characterize our lives are created here. And perhaps it's not strange that we are drawn to fantasies about things being different.

Fantasies about being alone. Floating in an empty space with just an umbilical cord connecting us to our surroundings.

That economic man doesn't match up to reality is one thing. We've known that for years. What's interesting is that we so dearly want him to align with reality.

Apparently we want to be like him. We want his self-sufficiency, his reason and the predictable universe that he inhabits. Most of all, we seem to be prepared to pay a high price for it.

What do we actually get out of so emphatically defending him against how things really are?

CHAPTER FOURTEEN

*In which we discover economic man's unforeseen
depths and fears*

In the 1500s and 1600s, the relationship between man and nature changed in the West. From a world view where people were seen as embedded in an often female, living and erratic cosmos, to one where men were seen as liberated, objective observers and conquerors of nature. From nature being seen as alive, in motion and organic (often in a frightening way), it became passive, dead and eventually mechanical.

Man was unbound from the whole: he became an independent individual tasked with conquering the world. Woman was constructed as the other: she should tether him to all that he didn't take with him.

Dependency, nature, the body, life.

He is reason. She is emotion. He is mind. She is body. He is independent. She is dependent. He is active. She is passive. He is selfish. She is self-sacrificing. He is hard. She is tender. He is calculating. She is unpredictable. He is rational. She is irrational. He is isolated. She is bound to everything. He is scientific. She is magical.

Men teach us that there are things worth dying for. Women teach us that there are things worth living for.

These are our performative roles. This is the dance itself. And it would be excellent if it were only that – a dance.

Actually, it matters less what men and women really do; we act in accordance with our assumptions rather than with the reality. Woman must somehow always take into account what is expected of her gender. And the same goes for men. But not quite in the same way.

When we talk about gender roles being dissolved it's rare to hear anyone suggest that young boys wear pink or that male bosses wear floral prints in order 'to be taken seriously'. That would look ridiculous, we say. However, a woman with a top job in the business world is still often expected to dress soberly. If she shows up in ruffles and a leather pencil skirt, she risks her colleagues' whispering. She has to dress neutrally: that is, in a masculine way. Adapt herself to a pre-existing structure organized around men's bodies. At the same time, she can't be too man-like. Still a woman – but a woman who gives a nod to the fact that she's doing something traditionally masculine.

And that's a difficult balancing act.

Our expectations of men are completely different. No one demands that Jamie Oliver adapt to a female gender role just because home cooking has traditionally been a female activity. The TV chef is immediately taken seriously by trading on his laddishness. Oliver doesn't chop basil. Oliver shoves the basil in a kitchen towel, bashes it on the table, grunts, conquers, forces the basil into submission – before he tosses it in the pot.

In the same way, a day care centre that wants to counteract

traditional gender roles will immediately be opposed to little girls wearing pink ballet outfits: no, we will not stand for these stereotypical clothes in gym class. Not in a socially progressive, democratic state. Here, we think that children should grow into free individuals, and so girls should not run around in ruffled pink ballet outfits during physical education. It reduces them to a gender stereotype that they might not be comfortable with.

But the same well-meaning pre-school teacher doesn't give a thought to the way boys dress. A pink ballet outfit is seen as a gender stereotype, the boys' equally traditional sporting kit is perceived as neutral.

Masculinity is almost always perceived this way. It's central to the construction of that gender identity.

Shakespeare's Prince Hamlet can embody a universal question. To be or not to be, is to be like him. We all learn to relate to him, even women. Hamlet's utterances are a human experience. Man is the norm and humanity becomes synonymous with masculinity.

To give birth is, however, not a human experience. It's a female experience. That's how they've taught us to view the world. The female experience is always separate from the universal. No one reads books about childbirth in order to understand human existence. We read Shakespeare. Or one of the great philosophers who write about how people spring from the earth like mushrooms and immediately start drafting social contracts with each other.

It's only woman who has a gender. Man is human. Only one sex exists. The other is a variable, a reflection, complementary.

*

In the world of economics we are all assumed to be rational, profiteering, selfish individuals. These are qualities that are always seen as traditionally masculine. So we also perceive them as neutral. They are not sexed – because man has never had a sex. Economic man becomes the only sex. At the same time the theory has always assumed that someone else stands for care, thoughtfulness and dependency. But all of this is invisible. If you want to be part of the story of economics, you have to be like economic man. And simultaneously what we call economics is always built on another story. All that which is excluded so economic man can be who he is. So he can say that there isn't anything else.

Women are worth as much as men.

Women complement men.

Women are just as good as men.

In each of these assertions, the woman is presented as a version of masculinity. Either the woman is 'like him'. Or she is 'in opposition to him'. But she is always in relation to him.

Either she is valuable because she is like a man – or she is valuable because she complements man. But it is always about the man. In one way of thinking, she can certainly work, research, fuck, burp, start a war, be rational and operate heavy machinery, just like him. That is, she should have the same rights and advantages that he has. But as soon as she stops being 'like him', she can no longer demand equality.

'No discrimination exists if pregnant men and pregnant women are treated the same,' it was ruled in the famous case *Geduldig v. Aiello* in the United States Supreme Court in 1974.

The case was about whether an insurance policy could specifically exclude pregnant women from its coverage. The court decided that it could. The policy wasn't excluding women. It was excluding 'pregnant persons'. That in all cases (and for a reason most people are aware of) these persons were women didn't have anything to do with it.

Woman can only gain entry to the categories that count economically and politically if she leaves her body on the other side. The idea that woman is valuable because she is 'like a man' implies a conditional liberation.

But in another way of thinking, that woman is valuable because she 'complements man' is more restrictive, if that's even possible.

Femininity is constructed in this case again as a variation of masculinity. Woman doesn't need to be like him, but is instead forced to be the kind wife who should provide the world with a counterweight to the hard, burgeoning markets. All the parts of the human experience that man hasn't been able to tolerate in himself he wants to experience in another way. Society has dictated for woman that she must be everything that he can't allow for himself: soft, vulnerable, the body, emotions, nature – the mystical dark side of the moon. She is forced to be body, emotion, nature, the subjective and the specific because he isn't. And in addition, she is said to be sentenced by her biology.

In this case, she's defined not by what he is, but by what he isn't.

But in both cases, by him.

Either woman must prove that she is like man, or she has to prove that she can complement him. It's never about her. Because there is only one sex.

*

When Richard Gere's alienated businessman takes Julia Roberts to the opera in the romantic comedy *Pretty Woman*, he is more interested in watching her reactions to *La Traviata* than in the performance itself. He isn't able to cry to Verdi. But he can watch her cry to Verdi. He needs her to access his own emotional life, and the only sure strategy that he can come up with to get closer to his feelings is to take the role as the observer of hers. She makes him feel alive. And suddenly he is convinced that he loves her.

By owning and conquering the woman, the man has been able to connect with the parts of himself that he otherwise denies. Dependency, emotions, context, pleasure and capitulation. But the woman is a person after all – not an essence. And really, he knows this.

'You sought a flower and found a fruit. You sought a spring and found a sea. You sought a woman and found a soul – you are disappointed,' wrote the poet Edith Södergran.

In an office high up in a 20-storey building, he works eighty hours a week, objectively making objective decisions of the utmost importance that have nothing to do with him. He left himself behind when he hung up his coat in the cloakroom that morning. There is no other way. He senses the smell of his own sickness in others' bodies, so he avoids them. Which doesn't mean that he doesn't sleep with them, because he does. He is helplessly drawn to women. Everything that he otherwise has to cut ties with he seeks in her. His childhood, his body, his sexuality and something else that he can't find the words for. But all that he finds, after a while, is another person who stares back at him with a fear that he has always suspected is in his eyes, too.

Today, every quality we call masculine belongs to the qualities that define economic behaviour. The distancing, rational and objective. He knows what he wants and goes out to get it. But not even men work this way. In spite of this, we have turned these qualities not only into an ideal, but also into a synonym for masculinity.

Deep down it is said that all of our actions can be reduced to one consciousness. The only sex.

Many have criticized economic man's one-dimensional perspective. He lacks depth, emotions, psychology and complexity, we think. He's a simple, selfish calculator. A caricature. Why do we keep dragging this paper doll around? It's ridiculous. What does he have to do with us?

But his critics are missing something essential. He isn't like us, but he clearly has emotions, depth, fears and dreams that we can completely identify with.

Economic man can't just be a simple paper doll, a run-of-the-mill psychopath or a random hallucination. Why, if he were, would we be so enchanted? Why would we so desperately try to align every part of existence with his view of the world, even though collected research shows that this model of human behaviour doesn't cohere with reality?

The desperation with which we want to align all parts of our lives with the fantasy says something about who we are. And what we are afraid of. This is what we have a hard time admitting to ourselves. Economic man's parodically simple behaviour doesn't mean that he isn't conjured from deep inner conflicts.

His identity is said to be completely independent of other

people. No man is an island, we say, and think that economic man's total self-sufficiency is laughable. But then we haven't understood his nature. You can't construct a human identity except in relation to others. And whether economic man likes it or not – this applies to him as well.

Because competition is central to his nature, his is an identity that is totally dependent on other people. Economic man is very much bound to others. But bound to them in a new way. Bound to them. Downright chained to them.

In competition.

If economic man doesn't compete, he is nothing, and to compete he needs other people. He doesn't live in a world without relationships. He lives in a world where all relationships are reduced to competition. He is aggressive and narcissistic. And he lives in conflict with himself. With nature and with other people. He thinks that conflict is the only thing that creates movement. Movement without risk. This is his life: filled with trials, tribulations and intense longing.

He is a man on the run.

The difference between the total production in a marriage and the sum of two independent people's production equals the profit in a marriage. This is measured (in many cases) by the vertical distance between the ever-elastic part of the demand curve for women and the supply curve of the same. These are the economic theories about love. Our fantasies cry out for independence and we dream desperately of control.

Let's assume that MI (the Man I) loves Ws (the Woman she) if her prosperity contributes to his utility function and perhaps also if MI values emotional and physical contact with

Ws. Then, it is clear that MI can benefit from a partnership with Ws. If they were together, it would have a greater impact on her prosperity (nuzzle her neck on a whim, reach the tins on the high shelf in the kitchen and hold her tight at night). Thereby, he'd also contribute to his own gain. The goods that measure 'contact' with Ws could indeed be produced more cheaply in a relationship than if MI and Ws lived each on their own. Even if Ws didn't love MI she'd benefit from being in a relationship with him. Because he loves her, her well-being is part of his utility function, and he can therefore be expected to transfer resources to her, which increases her profits, even if she doesn't love him back.

Economists describe romantic relationships like a rational calculation between two independent individuals. They do away with everything that has any bearing on the actual romantic relationship. Then they say that they have found the solution. Rational solutions for irrational problems. A chaos of specific ideas. Even our romantic relationships must conform to the cold, hard logic of the market. Both man and woman become economic man. We always have the full picture, we always keep a distance and stand a bit outside ourselves. Total control. And total security.

Economic man is the most seductive man on earth because he can take us away from all that frightens us. The body, emotion, dependency, insecurity and vulnerability. These don't exist in his world. Our bodies become human capital, dependency ceases to exist, and the world becomes predictable.

There is no such thing as difference. No vulnerability. And nothing to be afraid of.

That is why we cling to him. He helps us escape our fears.

Economic man transforms people's feelings into preferences. They become an impersonal set of desires. Orders from a menu that can be fulfilled or not fulfilled. If you have what it takes. But they are only preferences, nothing you ever have to get close to.

Feelings are not part of a person. In his world, feelings are something we sort, order, stack and arrange. Anger can help you in negotiations. Faking ecstasy in bed is part of a 'rational signalling model'. Love is when someone else's prosperity contributes to your utility function: it reduces conflict and therefore the costs of the relationships in which we choose to produce and raise children. And so you never need to manage your own feelings. That is, as long as you stay in economic man's world. And this world has its advantages. If we escape into it we don't have to deal with a lot of things we find difficult and confusing.

In the same way as your feelings become preferences, your body disappears. Economic man turns it into human capital. Suddenly it's not a part of you, but something you own. The body becomes currency that the individual can use in different ways and can invest in.

These economic theories place us outside our bodies. You can hire it out or sell it. Like any other venue. Change it, invest in it, and in the end, let it die. You are the owner, your body is capital, and this is your relationship.

Thus we become human in spite of our bodies, not through our bodies. To be reminded of the body is to be reminded that helplessness and total dependency are also a part of being human. That the body is born from another body and that it, as a wrinkled newborn, is at the mercy of its surroundings.

Dies without love. Expects everything and needs everything. Illness will push it into dependency. Ageing and death.

In economic man's world death is, on the other hand, a business decision. To shut it down or not to shut it down? Is my experienced gain greater than this pain? You don't need to think further on it. There is no meaning in death. And neither in life. The purpose is to create a world without purpose.

When we turn the body into human capital, the political consequences of the body disappear. Hands that are raised, legs that move, fingers that point, floors that are mopped, mouths that are fed. Our economy is built on bodies.

If the body was taken seriously as a starting point for the economy, it would have far-reaching consequences. A society organized around the shared needs of human bodies would be a very different society from the one we know now.

Hunger, cold, sickness, lack of healthcare and lack of food would be central economic concerns. Not like today: unfortunate by-products of the one and only system.

Our economic theories refuse to accept the reality of the body and flee as far from it as they can. That people are born small and die fragile, and that skin cut with a sharp object will bleed no matter who you are, no matter where you come from, no matter what you earn and no matter where you live. What we have in common starts with the body. We shiver when we are cold, sweat when we run, cry out when we come and cry out when we give birth. It's through the body that we can reach other people. So, economic man eradicates it. Pretends it doesn't exist. We observe it from the outside as if it were foreign capital.

And we are alone.

*

In flight from the body and from emotions, economic man is also fleeing dependency. And this of course is connected. It's often through the body that dependency finds its expression. Economic man never needs: he just wants. And if we are like him, we'll never need to feel left out and never have to ask for anything. Never feel that we aren't deserving and never need to deal with the consequences: never worry that we can't take something without being able to pay it back.

In economic man's world there is nothing like this. All accounts are balanced. His is the only concept of freedom that he can imagine.

And he has come up with it himself.

Economic man is a flight from insecurity. You can count on everything. Everything is predictable. You can calculate the volume of a ball by dividing it into smaller and smaller rectangles. Just like life. The movements of populations and the forces that drive them. Everything occurs according to abstract laws. And he is a flight from weakness. We are masters of a universe that obeys our every nod. In the story of economics, this seems to be the only purpose the world has. The market always does what you want it to, pushes out those who deserve it and crawls after those who are worthy.

The story of economic man perpetuates the myth of a person as an all-knowing, rational subject. Master of his life. Master of the world. When we engage with economics, these are the clothes that we wear. Everything else falls away. Sex, background, history, body and context. Economic man is a flight from difference. We become not just one and the same sex but one and the same person. So of course it's easy to quantify us and predict how we'll behave.

Economic man is not a paper doll. He is not a caricature. And he is not simple in the least. He is a symptom of the parts of reality that he tries to exterminate. The body, emotions, dependency, insecurity and vulnerability. The parts of reality that for thousands of years society has told woman she belongs to. He tells us they don't exist.

Because he can't handle it.

He flees, he agonizes, and we identify with the dizzying depth of his fears. And that's why we have been seduced.

Economic theory becomes a place to hide. A place where society tells stories about itself. The things we need. The things we just hum along to.

The only sex. The only choice. And the only world.

CHAPTER FIFTEEN

*In which we see that the greatest story of our time
only has one sex*

In one of her poems, Muriel Rukeyser revisits the Greek myth of King Oedipus. He who it was foretold would accidentally kill his father and marry his mother and who solved the mysterious riddle of the Sphinx.

Many years later, after he had killed his father and married his mother and put out his own eyes in shame, Oedipus bumped into the Sphinx again, the one whose famous riddle he had solved.

'You answered the riddle wrong that time,' she said. 'That's why things went the way they did.'

'How do you mean?' wondered the old and blinded Oedipus. 'I answered correctly. I was the first who had ever given the correct answer – that was the whole point of that part of the story.'

'No,' said the Sphinx, 'when I asked what walks on four legs in the morning, two at noon and three in the evening, you answered, Man. You said that man walks on four legs in the morning of his life, two as an adult and three legs with a cane in the twilight of his life. You said nothing about woman.'

'But,' Oedipus protested, 'when you say Man, you include women, too. Everyone knows that.'

'That's what you think,' answered the Sphinx.

Western culture is full of dichotomies: are you body or soul, emotion or reason, nature or culture, subjective or objective, specific or universal? Essentially: are you feminine or masculine? All that economic man has been defined as not being – these are the aspects of existence that we traditionally attribute to the woman.

Body, emotion, dependency and vulnerability.

In one single person we have managed to collect all the characteristics that we for centuries have called 'masculine'. Economists say this is a coincidence. Economic man only happens to come across that way. And anyway, we can fit women into the model if we want. Essentially all people can be reduced to this abstract, rational economic consciousness. Irrespective of sex, irrespective of race, irrespective of culture, irrespective of age, irrespective of social status.

What is this if not equality?

Actually, the idea of economic man is an efficient way of excluding women. We have historically allocated women certain activities and said that she must do them because she is a woman. Then we create an economic theory that states that these activities have no economic meaning. We tell the woman that she must embody certain driving forces so that the man's society can function: care, empathy, altruism, thoughtfulness. At the same time we'll say that the economy is the only thing that matters, really.

Economic theory is raised up as supreme logic in society,

but the driving forces that we have coded as feminine are of course still there – otherwise the whole thing wouldn't cohere.

We have created an economic language that makes it impossible to talk about the whole.

The only thing we can talk about is economic man. If we want to be able to talk about Adam Smith's mother, we have to turn her into economic man. If we want to talk about art, we have to turn sculptures, paintings – and even the feelings you have when you view them – into goods in a marketplace. If we want to be able to talk about our relationships, we have to turn them into relationships of competition.

And what doesn't fit into the models, well, that's its own problem.

Economic man's primary characteristic is that he is not a woman. Economics only has one sex. Woman can choose between trying to be him or being his opposite. Complement and balance his hard logic of rationality and self-interest. She has chosen it herself. Because everything we do is the result of free will.

The interesting part isn't what the theory says about women but rather what can be said about women in a theory.

Today the standard theories of economics maintain that economic outcomes are gender neutral. And they look incredibly neutral when they are expressed as abstract mathematics. But economists saying that sex lacks importance doesn't prevent people, because of their sex, from having different structural relationships to production, reproduction and consumption in society.

Women have worse access to education and technology.

Worse access to clean water. Worse access to healthcare. Worse access to credit. Worse access to the financial markets. Have a harder time getting loans. Have a harder time starting businesses. Worse working conditions. Worse wages. Less secure employment. Worse understanding of their rights and worse information about what the law says.

Sex matters in a world where 20% of all women live below the international poverty line, while at the same time women are virtually absent from the new global super-elite that has been created in the upper stratospheres of the global economy. An elite that has secured ever greater influence over our economic and political systems.

Sex matters in a world where women have lower wages, worse working conditions and perform most of the unpaid work, work that is undervalued and excluded from the statistics we use to measure economic performance.

Sex matters in a world where norms, cultures and values restrict women just because they are women. Even though economists claim that these norms, cultures and values aren't economically relevant, and assert that economics itself is totally free from said norms, cultures and values. A neutral expression of the innermost truth about mankind.

In short.

That men and women have different structural positions in the economy means that economic policies impact men and women in different ways. And economic theory, which is blind to this, can't deal with it and can't even measure it.

One of the problems with the patriarchy is that it leads to insufficient ways of measuring the economy. And measurements are important.

Those who think the market alone will solve all our problems don't need statistics. They can satisfy themselves by saying the economic theories are impressive works of art: mathematical depictions of a myth that happens to turn us on. Those who, on the other hand, want to use the economy to achieve social goals have to understand how the economy works. If you want to have an accurate picture of the market you can't, for example, ignore what half of the world's population is doing half of the time.

If women's unpaid work isn't included in economic models, we'll never understand how their unrecognized labour is linked to poverty and inequality between the sexes.

And if you want to understand why a country develops in the way that it does, you can't ignore all its driving forces bar self-interest, greed and fear.

Economic theory gives us a way to look at the world and says it can diagnose a country's problems, formulate conditions for its public debates, predict how it will develop and prescribe remedies to cure it. Precisely because the theory insists that it holds the truth about human nature.

If economics is supposed to help solve mankind's problems, it can't continue to stare blindly at a masculine fantasy world where there is only one sex.

Economists believe that their role is to equip society with the necessary knowledge to tend to the economic system. But the closest predecessors of today's economists are not scientists like Albert Einstein or Isaac Newton. Economists are, more rightly, the heirs of theologists like Thomas Aquinas and Martin Luther, as Robert H. Nelson asserts in the book *Economics as*

Religion. According to Nelson, who is himself an economist, the task of economists has been to function as a modern-day priesthood that spreads the belief that economic progress is the route to salvation.

The founders of economic science viewed the field in explicitly messianic terms. Evil, pain and even death itself were largely a consequence of material scarcity in the world. We stole because we were hungry, suffered when we didn't have enough money, and in many cases died because we didn't have the resources to survive.

Economic science believed that the only things that could lift the world out of this state were correctly formulated, correctly lived and correctly implemented principles for society. Economists saw it as their task to spread these values and therewith offer the world a path to salvation. Today we know it's not that simple:

People can die of loneliness – not just of lack of food or water.

An infant who no one picks up or touches won't survive. Even if its material needs are met.

And rich people steal, too. Just ask the great racketeer Bernard Madoff.

Human society, after a certain point, cannot be made happier as a result of economic growth.

But Robert H. Nelson sees neither this nor modern economics' inability to describe reality as a problem. Economic man may be a myth. But he is a useful myth, because he gets us to focus on the right things.

Believing that economics is a science fulfils an important economic function, according to Robert H. Nelson. Whether economic theories of how people and markets work are true or not, they legitimate and organize society around a set of values that are needed for the economy to grow.

Nelson looks back on his own time as a political adviser. He asserts that it was precisely this that was his role: he tried to encourage decision-makers to increasingly make decisions based on an economic value system. Because he believed that economic values were the best values for society. And he still believes this.

Like most missionaries, some economists believe that reality is only part of the picture. Even if God doesn't exist, many priests have done good in the world. Economic theories are demonstrably wrong in how they describe the world and people, says Nelson, but these false theories have done a lot of good for society. They have been a basis for development over the last 200 years.

Our western perspective that religion must 'make claims to truth' in order for us to believe in it is precisely a perspective, he writes. Whether a religion is worth practising or not doesn't have to be contingent on how close to the truth it lies – it should also be judged on the kind of world it creates.

Today economic science is the dominant religion in the western world. As long as we continue to believe in the power of economics there will be a continuing demand for a priestly class that can produce appropriate religious interpretation and symbolism.

And even if economists don't teach us very much about how the economy works in reality, the fictional picture they paint of the market is an admirable work of art. Furthermore, it has given us a language with which to discuss economic questions. That is a feat in itself, writes Nelson.

And maybe he has a point. Religion or not, regardless of which complicated mathematical models economic theory makes use of, it always carries its values with it. Diluted with facts, moral assumptions and doctrines, it creates what we today call economic logic. Of course data about inflation, unemployment and everything else that economists have compiled and analysed have contributed to society developing in the extraordinary way that it has. But economic science has seldom stopped at that.

It has asserted that it is so much more, and somewhere along the way, things went wrong.

There is no formal economic church, there are no ordained high priests, no official decrees identifying the holy texts – there is not even a definitive definition of what economic theory is. But the belief that the market's logic lives in human nature is one that we carry with us every day. It has worked its way deeper and deeper into our culture. We are encouraged to turn to it again and again, and in ever more areas of life. The discussion about economic man is therefore a question for each and every one of us. It is not only about how economics can form hypotheses that better cohere with reality, thereby preventing itself from contributing to the collapse of the world economy. Saving face. And moving on.

The logic of the market is excellent when deciding which sort of lipstick should be produced, for whom it should be produced, in which colours it should be produced and what it should cost. But American satirist H. L. Mencken's observation that on noticing that roses smell better than cabbage, you can't conclude that they will make better soup can also be applied to the logic of the market. Just because it works well in some areas doesn't mean it should be applied to all areas. Unfortunately, applying the logic of the market to everything has largely become the project of economists in recent decades.

What we call economic theory is the formal version of the dominant world view in our society. The greatest story of our time: who we are, why we are here and the reason we do what we do.

And the person in this story, economic man? His defining characteristic is that he is not a woman.

CHAPTER SIXTEEN

In which we will see that every society suffers in line with its bullshit. And we say goodbye.

You might think it silly that the world's third-largest indoor snow park is in Dubai. On the Persian Gulf. On the 25th parallel north. The temperature outside is around forty degrees Celsius in the dry, windy summer months. In the winter it goes down to twenty-three.

The skiing facility is open at least twelve hours a day, seven days a week and covers 22,500 square meters. Six thousand tonnes of snow are used on five different slopes. The longest is 400 metres and has a sixty-metre drop. It is the world's only indoor black run.

The difference between the temperature outside and the temperature inside is on average thirty-two degrees. You don't want to know how much energy it takes to cool the place down. Still we call it economically rational. If we think about it at all. Building a ski slope in the middle of the desert? Yes, well, if people want to pay for it, why not? That's the only question we know how to ask.

Is the economy fair? Does economics increase the quality of life? Does the economy waste human capacity? Does the economy create enough security? Does the economy waste the world's resources? Does the economy create enough opportunities for meaningful work? None of those questions can be asked within today's dominant economic doctrines.

If you question economics, you question your inner nature. And then you're insulting yourself. So you keep quiet.

Economics today creates appetites instead of solutions. The western world swells with obesity while others starve. The rich wander about like gods in their own nightmares. Or go skiing in the desert. You don't even have to be particularly rich to do that. Those who once were starving now have access to chips, Coca-Cola, trans fats and refined sugars, but they are still disenfranchized. It is said that when Mahatma Gandhi was asked what he thought about western civilization, he answered that yes, it would be a good idea. The bank man's bonuses and the oligarch's billions are natural phenomena. Someone has to pull away from the masses – or else we'll all become poorer. After the crash Icelandic banks lost 100 billion dollars. The country's GDP had only ever amounted to thirteen billion dollars in total. An island with chronic inflation, a small currency and no natural resources to speak of: fish and warm water. Its economy was a third of Luxembourg's. Well, they should be grateful they were allowed to take part in the financial party. Just like ugly girls should be grateful. Enjoy, swallow and don't complain when it's over. Economists can pull the same explanations from their hats every time. Dream worlds of total social exclusion and endless consumerism grow where they can be left in peace, at a safe distance from the poverty and environmental destruction they spread around themselves. Alternative universes for privileged human life forms. The stock market rises and the stock market falls. Countries devalue and currencies ripple. The market's movements are monitored minute by minute. Some people always walk in threadbare shoes. And you arrange your preferences to avoid meeting them. It's no longer possible to see further into the future than one desire at a time. History has ended and individual freedom has taken over.

There is no alternative.

It's not just that every aspect of economic man's personality overlaps with every trait throughout history that we've come to call masculine. These traits are also those which we have understood to be superior to and worthy of dominating that which we call feminine.

The soul is more refined than the body and we associate the soul with him. Reason is more refined than emotion, and we associate reason with him. Universal is better than specific, and we associate the universal with him.

Objective is better than subjective, and we associate objectivity with man – he who can stand outside a situation, observing coolly and unaffected by what he sees. Culture is more refined than nature and we associate culture with him. She is untamed nature; he worships her as much as he is frightened by her.

Woman is body, she is earth and she is passive. She is dependent, she is nature and man is the opposite. He fertilizes her, he chastens her, he ploughs her and extracts from her. He fills her with meaning and sets her in motion.

On his journey, Homer's hero Odysseus overcomes nature, myth and the siren song of female sexuality in order to return home and re-establish patriarchal power over his wife in Ithaca. The entire self-perception of the West is built around these stories. We have learned to view the sexes as a dichotomy and that's the way it is in many traditions. But not in all.

In Lao Tzu's classical work *Tao Te Ching*, written in China in around 600 BC, yin and yang's movements beget each other. The feminine and masculine are energies that follow each other in a circular motion in which neither a hierarchy nor a dichotomy can take shape. In the *Daodejing*, yin and yang are described not as either/or, which is the traditional patriarchal view of these forces, but in many ways as a path that moves past dichotomies. That which is traditionally called 'feminine', or yin, is free and can be embraced by all people, irrespective of sex. The whole is constantly in a process of change and creation – nothing is fixed or locked.

But this didn't become the dominant view of the sexes in the world.

What the feminine has been associated with has almost always been constructed as that which must be subordinate to the masculine. Nature should be tamed by culture, the body should be chastened by the soul. Those who are autonomous should take care of those who are dependent. The active should penetrate the passive. The man produces. The woman consumes. That's why he should make the decisions. It explains itself.

These economic theories are a continuation of the same story. Economic man dominates through the force of his masculinity. A company's profits can in the same way be allowed to dominate all other ambitions in the economy and within the firm itself. Justice, equality, care, the environment, trust, physical and mental health are subordinate. Because there is an economic theory that can justify it. That can explain why nothing else is possible. Even though deep down we know it's madness.

So, instead of seeing justice, equality, care, the environment, trust, physical and mental health as fundamental parts of the equation that creates economic value, they are construed as something that is in opposition to it.

It's one thing to organize the economy so that the quality of life will continue to rise. It's another thing to subordinate all of society's values to profit and competition.

The world's resources are limited, we say. Nature is static, stingy and hostile and therefore we must compete with each other. From this competition is born the energy that fuels the economic system. That puts your dinner on the table and decides the price of everything from waffles to test tube babies.

The most famous definition of economics was made by Lionel Robbins in 1932. Economics was, according to him, 'the science which studies human behaviour as a relationship between ends and scarce means which have alternative uses'. The characters are stingy, hostile nature playing against a person with unlimited appetite and total freedom of choice. The story touches on our old conceptions about man, whose reason dominates and conquers feminine nature. That which he both desires and fears.

How different the world would be, the economist Julie Nelson muses, if we had, for example, defined economics as 'the science which studies how humans satisfy the requirements and enjoy the delights of life using the free gifts of nature'.

Here nature isn't a counterpart but a given. It's flexible, generous and friendly. Our relationship to it isn't grab-everything-you-can-carry-or-eat, but nature as part of the same whole that we ourselves are part of.

We can criticize economic man as much as we like. As long as we can't see that he is a gendered theory of the world based on our collective fear of the 'female' we will never be free.

As a society, after thousands of years of the oppression of women, we can wholly identify with him. The depth of his feelings. Fear of vulnerability, of nature, of emotion, of dependency, of the cyclical and of everything we can't understand. This is the very story of our society. The desperate flight from parts of our humanity that we refuse to acknowledge.

And if we continue to flee, we need economic man. More than the air we breathe.

How we choose to view mankind and her actions within the economy says a lot about how we see ourselves.

Economic phenomena always have their roots in people's dealings: going to the store, buying underwear, planning the erection of a new bridge, planting a tree, sneaking a glance at our neighbour and wishing we had the same car. But economists almost always present these dealings on a consolidated statistical level: market price, a nation's GDP, consumer spending and so forth.

This statistical reality is supposed to come out of what the players are doing on a micro level, and economists therefore demand to have some sort of idea of how people act economically. Who is that person, why is she doing what she is doing – in what way does it relate to the aggregated story about her and all the others who create the GDP's curve on page four of the Minister of Finance's PowerPoint presentation?

This is one of the problems with this story. And there are more.

Every collection of suppositions about mankind within economics will always in some way be a simplification. Do we really need to know who we are to understand the economy? Maybe not. But we definitely can't understand the economy by doing everything in our power to run away from precisely that question.

And that's the very function of economic man. To flee. To deny the body, emotion, dependency and context. As well as the responsibility for the whole that we are part of. All that we refuse to accept in the humanity we belong to.

Dependency has for centuries been seen as shameful. It was something that slaves and women were. When working-class men demanded the right to vote they did it by arguing that they were indeed independent. Before, dependency had been defined through ownership. Those who were owners were independent. Those who worked for someone else were dependent.

But the workers' movement redefined that which was previously called wage-slavery as a source of pride. Independence came to be defined as having a job with a salary that could support a family. Then one was doing one's duty. So one could also demand rights.

Woman, on the other hand, couldn't do this – because she was still dependent.

That for working-class men to be 'independent' by working full-time they had to depend on women to take care of the home was not a part of this history. Just as Adam Smith failed to tell us about his mother.

What counts as dependency and who is seen as a parasite on whom has always been a political question. Does Adam Smith need his mother, or does she need him?

The truth is we are all dependent and therefore society's task cannot be to separate those who produce from those who consume. We are all accountable to each other and to ourselves. Whatever else we tell ourselves, we can't escape the fact that we are still a part of the whole. And we need a way to talk about this.

Today mankind's true experience of itself has no place in economics. Our standard economic theories are based on a fictional character whose foremost characteristic is that he isn't a woman.

One would think that economists would devote themselves to finding solutions for the very complex problems that mankind is facing. Instead they stare blindly at their own assumptions about a masculine nature that not even men possess.

We govern the world from a place of not knowing who we are.

It is said that everything should be divided into its smallest part and that it will only be intelligible when it's divorced from everything else in a relationship of competition. This world view makes it difficult to address the things that really matter.

Economic theories don't help us understand either what

our day-to-day choices mean for the whole and for society or what they'll mean for the future that we will leave behind us one day, no matter how much we pretend that our actions are isolated impulses in a void.

Economists should help us understand who we are by creating tools and methods for organizing a society with room for the entire human experience. Together with others, as part of the whole, the only unit through which we become intelligible. Intelligible to ourselves, to others and, for that matter, even to mathematical formulas.

If we better understood our desires, we would probably see that they can't be satisfied in the way that we imagine. Overworked. Over-stimulated. Overspent. Without an alternative and yet with all the choice in the world. Credit, debt, fear and greed. Just because you're running doesn't mean you're not running in circles. Faster and faster. A sole dream of total separation. The world ends where it began. Thrashing around and crying for more. Everyone is trying to get you. That's why you do as they say. That's why you wake up in the morning. That's why you pay the bills and save the receipts. Expectations are just trapped pain. A weak affirmation that lets the darkness in. If you want to get to the honey, you don't kill all the bees. The market lives in human nature. And every society suffers in line with its own bullshit.

Economics should help us rise above fear and greed. It should not exploit these feelings.

Economic science should be about how one turns a social vision into a modern economic system.

It should be a tool to create opportunities for human and

social development. Not just address our fears as they are expressed as demand in the market.

It should be devoted to concrete questions that are important for humanity. Not to abstract analyses of hypothetical choices.

It should see people as reasonable beings. Not as wagons hooked to the consequences of an unavoidable, coercive rationality. It should see people as embedded in society. Not as individuals whose core never changes and who float in a vacuum at an arm's length from each other.

It should see relationships as fundamental for us to even be able to individuate ourselves. Not as something that can be reduced to competition, profit, loss, buying low, selling high and calculating who won.

It should see a person as someone who acts according to her bonds with others. Not just out of self-interest and the denial of all context and power relationships.

It should not see self-interest and altruism as opposites – because it should no longer view the surrounding world as something that is in opposition to one's self.

Why are you unhappy? wrote the poet Wei Wu Wei.
 Because 99.9%
 Of everything you think,
 And of everything you do,
 Is for yourself—
 And there isn't one

Instead of fleeing vulnerability, we could admit it's part of being human. Everything we have in common starts in the body.

Instead of construing emotions as the opposite of reason, we could take an interest in how people actually make decisions.

Instead of reducing all people to one and the same abstract consciousness, we could accept difference.

Our relationships wouldn't need to be reduced to competition. Nature wouldn't have to be a hostile counterpart. We could admit that the whole is greater than the sum of its parts. That the world isn't a machine or an elaborate mechanical performance. And then we could free ourselves of economic man. Cries of futility are expressed in many ways, but this doesn't have to be one of them. The purpose of this journey could change. We could go from trying to own the world to trying to feel at home in it.

And here's the difference. To own is to possess. To wrap your hands around a dead thing and say 'This is mine'. When you feel at home, you never need to say that this is mine.

Because you know that it isn't.

And that's when you take off your shoes – prepared to stay a while.

EPILOGUE

She was called Margaret Douglas, Adam Smith's mother. An ageing, serious woman, dressed mostly in black, she sits in the corner of a room in a red armchair, her right hand resting on a book that she has apparently just shut. The year is 1778, and she is 84 years old. Her portrait was painted by Conrad Metz the same year that Adam Smith's household packed up and moved to Edinburgh.

Today it hangs in the Kirkcaldy Galleries in Fife.

Margaret Douglas was born in September 1694, the fifth child of a noble Scottish family. She grew up in Strathenry Castle, 125 miles from Kirkcaldy. Her father, Robert Douglas, was a member of the Scottish Parliament and an important man. His daughter Margaret married Adam Smith senior at the age of twenty-six. She was fifteen years his junior.

They spent just over two years together.

In January 1723 Adam Smith senior dies. Six months later his son Adam is born. Margaret Douglas never remarries.

She is a widow at twenty-eight and at the age of two Adam Smith inherits his father's estate. His mother can only lay claim to one third of the inheritance. From this point onwards, she's essentially dependent on her son for money.

He also remains dependent on her until her death.

'His mother herself was from first to last the heart of

Smith's life,' John Rae wrote in his biography of Adam Smith.

It's Margaret Douglas who tends to Adam Smith's household, almost irrespective of where he moves to, and for a long time she does this with one of Adam's cousins, Janet Douglas, about whom future generations will know even less about. All we know is that she was important. In 1788, as Janet Douglas lies on her deathbed, Adam Smith writes a letter to a friend: 'She will leave me one of the most destitute and helpless men in Scotland.'

In his economic theories, however, there is no trace of these insights. As feminist economist Edith Kuiper points out, in contrast even to his contemporary philosophers, women are almost entirely absent from Adam Smith's thinking.

It hasn't been the intention of this book to explain why.

Neither do I, as the author, want to be too hard on Adam Smith.

Virginia Woolf couldn't cook either.

Karl Marx had a housekeeper with whom he also had sex. That's not the point. The point is that the discipline and lineage of thought that Adam Smith originated omitted something fundamental when Adam Smith forgot about his mother.

As perhaps one does.

But as economics has become ever more important over the centuries this fundamental mistake has had far-reaching consequences.

The great financial crisis of 2008 came and went without the economic story it was built on being challenged in the way that so many believed was inevitable. The ideas didn't fall along with the banks. This book has argued that this was partly because we didn't understand how thoroughly economic man had seduced us.

We cannot challenge economic man without feminism, and we can hardly change anything of importance today without challenging economic man.

Margaret Douglas is the missing piece of the puzzle.

But it doesn't necessarily follow that when you find the missing piece the solution will become clear.

'There is no such thing as a free lunch' is one of the most often-quoted truths in economics.

To this it should be added: there is no such thing as free care.

If society doesn't provide childcare that we all contribute to, then someone else will have to provide it. And that someone is most often a woman.

Today, Margaret Douglas is the woman who reduces her hours at work to care for her grandchildren. She does this because she loves them and because there isn't any other solution. Her daughter and her son-in-law have their own jobs to go to. There's no chance their family could survive on one salary, when they can barely manage on two.

It's usually women who reduce their working hours to care for their offspring and who, as a result, lose out on economic security, pension contributions and future earnings.

And it's our welfare, tax and pension systems that haven't been built to compensate them for this work or even to take it into account.

Women's responsibility for care is presented as a free choice, and we reason that when you make a choice out of your own free will, you have to accept the consequences.

Everything from the Scandinavian welfare states to our neoliberal economies is built on women doing certain kinds of jobs in the workforce at a very low cost. It's a formula founded on the fact that only a few fields were once open to women. If you wanted to have a career as a woman, you could mainly choose between becoming a nurse or becoming a teacher. Health and education systems could therefore recruit highly educated, motivated and brilliant women without a problem.

But would Florence Nightingale have become a nurse today?

Probably not.

She'd have become a doctor, a researcher, a health economist or a professor of statistics.

And that would have been excellent.

But who would be the nurse?

Each year, thousands of British nurses leave Great Britain. They move to countries where the salaries are higher and the conditions are better.

When it's not a given that women perform a certain kind of work, it's harder to recruit them. And this is work that's often related to care, to duty, nursing the sick, children and the ageing.

Can today's problems in healthcare and education even be discussed without this perspective?

The modern-day Margaret Douglas often takes care both of the children and of her own or her partner's sick parents. Seventeen per cent of unemployed British women quit their last job in order to care for someone else.

For men, that figure is one per cent.

In many countries stay-at-home mums have almost exclusively become a phenomenon of the upper and lower levels of society.

The super rich thrive on one salary, while poor women in countries with low wages and high childcare costs literally can't afford to work.

British society is an example of this. Poor mothers who aren't working for a living are given benefits so that they can stay at home, but then they are also mocked and made to feel guilty for not supporting themselves.

When the minimum wage doesn't cover the costs of childcare by a long shot, families are confronted with an equation that can't be solved.

Conservative politicians rage against benefits, but at the same time they don't want to provide universal childcare.

In turn, those on the Left have a hard time talking about reliance on benefits at all.

The result is welfare states that haven't adapted to an almost totally transformed social reality.

We tell ourselves that we value the next generation more than almost anything else in our world, but we don't back that up with investment.

European women say that they want to have on average 2.36 children.

In reality they give birth to around 1.7.

What causes this gap?

What's preventing women in Europe from having the number of children that they want to have?

The traditional family model – Dad at work and Mum at home – is no recipe for high birth rates. In fact, lots of evidence points to the contrary. Since the mid-1990s the lowest fertility levels in Europe have been found in the countries that also have the lowest rates of female participation in the labour force.

When society doesn't help or encourage women to combine having children with having paid work, fewer children are born. When women are forced to choose between a career and children, many women choose the career.

And the countries where this happens, such as Germany, Italy and Japan, all face serious economic problems.

When women, as happens in many European countries, only give birth to 1.5 children each, that means the population will be reduced. Ever fewer will have to support ever more. Society doesn't equal out over generations. To solve the problem, you have to either cut down on benefits or raise taxes. You have to either open the borders and try to attract young people from other countries, or get your own people to retire later.

The question of how it could be possible to combine family with work outside the home isn't a privileged complaint from a female elite that wants to have it all. It is an enormous challenge that affects the entire economy and the entire population.

In the meantime, it's true that the conversation about balancing a career and a child is often about women who have a career.

It's less frequently about men, which it should be.

And it's even less frequently about women who don't have a career.

That is, about women who only have a job.

In March 2014 Shanesha Taylor was arrested by the police in Arizona. The single mother had left her children alone in a car for forty-five minutes; a two-year-old and a six-month-old baby sat there in the heat. Thankfully nothing happened to them, but Shanesha Taylor was arrested for having endangered their lives.

Her story spread across the USA.

Not because it was unusual, but because the reason she left her children in their car seats was that she was going to a job interview.

She was homeless and unemployed and had arranged for a sitter so she could go to the interview. It was for a job that she believed was one of the few chances she had to improve her family's economic situation.

But then the sitter cancelled.

So she chose to leave her children in the car.

This is what work–life balance means for millions of women.

'Career' means zero-hour contracts, irregular shifts and nervously ringing the boss every morning to check if there's work.

In the era leading up to the financial crisis of 2008 many economies started to take the shape of an hourglass. Jobs were being created among the glass and steel palaces of the banks at the top, as well as in an ever-expanding and increasingly insecure service sector at the bottom. The jobs in this latter sector were often exactly the kind of work that previously had been done for free by women in the home. Now it had been transferred to the market, but the work was poorly paid and irregular; it went with the flow of migration that, through its movement across the globe, ensured that our societies still hung together in spite of their intrinsic impossibility.

If you want to understand why we are experiencing an

increase in economic inequality, you have to understand the feminist perspective of economics: how Adam Smith got his dinner, and why this was of economic importance.

The discussion about economics has indeed changed since the crisis of 2008, and we are in the process of widening our view of what it is. Many people are expressing the ideas that are put forward in this book, albeit in different ways and with different starting points.

As the author, I have attempted to contribute my version. A story about how economic man was a way to flee from large parts of our humanity and how we now find ourselves in between world views and en route to losing our religion.

Feminism's best-kept secret is just how necessary a feminist perspective is in the search for a solution to our mainstream economic problems. It is involved in everything from inequality to population growth to benefits to the environment and the care crunch that will soon face many ageing societies. Feminism is about so much more than 'rights for women'. So far only half of the feminist revolution has happened. We have added women and stirred. The next step is to realize what a massive shift this has been, and to actually change our societies, economies and politics to fit the new world we have created. Wave economic man off from the platform and then build an economy and a society with room for a greater spectrum of what it means to be a human.

We don't need to call it a revolution; rather, it could be termed an improvement.

The epilogue to this story has been written in a garden in North London against greenish-blue garden furniture, the climbing roses in bloom, and in hope of exactly that.

NOTES

PROLOGUE

2   *Said Christine Lagarde in 2010, when she was still France's Minister of Finance*: see Lagarde, 2010

3   *And there are studies that show that men with higher testosterone levels are more prone to taking risks*: see Croson and Gneezy, 2009.

3   *What is the connection between the business cycle and the menstrual cycle?*: see Pearson and Schipper, 2013.

3   *Norms and ideas about what your sex is in relation to the so-called opposite sex seem to matter*: see Booth, Cardone-Sosac and Nolena, 2014.

5   *Women with less education have more children, and they have them a lot younger*: see Wolf, 2013, chapter 2.

5   *But even in these world-renowned welfare states women earn less than men: women's wages, recalculated as full-time salaries, are on average around 17 per cent lower than men's in Sweden. The difference has been about the same for the last twenty years*: see Statistics Sweden, 2004.

5   *The number of women in senior management positions in business is small compared with many other countries*: when countries are ranked according to how many woman hold senior management positions in the business world,

Sweden came in 25th, Finland was in 13th place, with Denmark in 37th place. Grant Thornton International Business Report 2012.

CHAPTER ONE

8   *Economics has been described as the science of how you conserve love*: see McCloskey, 2000, p. 13.

9   *What's 100 metres long, moves at a snail's pace and lives only on cabbage?*: A joke that appeared in the former Soviet Union.

9   *'The first principle of economics is that every agent is actuated only by self-interest'*: Edgeworth, 1967, p. 16.

9   *The modern economy was built on 'the granite of self-interest'*: Stigler, 1971, p. 265.

10   *Morality represents the way we would like the world to work, economists tell us how it actually does work*: from the foreword to *Freakonomics*.

10   *Adam Smith coined the term, but it's the economists since him who popularized it*: the expression 'the invisible hand' appears only one time in *The Wealth of Nations* and then in relation to import restrictions (see *The Wealth of Nations*, Book IV, Chapter 2).

12   *'I can calculate the motion of heavenly bodies but not the madness of people'*: attributed to Newton. The quotation appears for the first time in Henry Richard Fox Bourne's book *The Romance of Trade* from 1871.

13   *If you understand the individual, you understand everything, they thought*: see, for example, Davis, 2003.

14   *'What really interests me is whether God had any choice in the creation of the world'*: among others, quoted in Hawking, 1993, p. 113.

14 *Economic theory is 'a body of generalization whose substantial accuracy and importance are open to question only by the ignorant or the perverse'*: Robbins, p. 1.

15 *'There is no alternative,' said Margaret Thatcher*: the slogan was often used by British prime minister Margaret Thatcher. 'There is no alternative' is also expressed as the acronym TINA.

15 *The market dictates what it is worth for an investment bank to crash straight into the taxpayers reserves (70 million dollars a year)*: Richard S. Fuld Jr, CEO for Lehman Brothers, is estimated to have earned 500 million dollars between 2000 and 2007. See also Bebchuk, Cohen and Spamann, 2010.

15 *And what it is worth to hold an eighty-seven-year-old woman's anxious hand as she takes her last 700 breaths in a Scandinavian welfare state (ninety-six krona – around eight pounds – an hour)*: Approximately the lowest wage for enrolled nurses.

16 *The father of economics lived with his mother for most of his life*: see Phillipson, 2010.

16 *In the GDP calculation, which measures the total economic activity in a country, she isn't counted*: for more on women and the GDP, see Waring, 1999.

16 *The French author and feminist Simone de Beauvoir described woman as 'the second sex'*: see de Beauvoir, 2006.

17 *Today it is sometimes pointed out that the economy isn't just built with an 'invisible hand', it is also built with an 'invisible heart'*: see Folbre, 2001.

CHAPTER TWO

18 *A. A. Milne, the author of the* Winnie the Pooh *books, noted*: Milne, 2004, pp. 14–16.

18 *Most students of economics have heard their professor retell Daniel Defoe's 1719 novel in some way*: see, for example, Grapard and Hewitson, 2011.

19 *In the novel, Robinson Crusoe is born in York, England*: Defoe, 1992.

20 *The tools and materials are made by others even if they are far away,* for feminist discus-sion about Robinson Crusoe as economic man see <copy to follow>

21 *The Irish writer James Joyce described Robinson*: see Joyce, 1964, pp. 24–25.

21 Ceteris paribus, *economics professors sermonize*: for a defini-tion, see, for example, Marshall, 1920, book V, chapter V.

23 *Thus was born the model of human behaviour that has defined economic thought since then*: it was John Stuart Mill who first used the term 'the economic man'. The term is also associated with thinkers from the 1700s such as Adam Smith, but it only started to be widely used in the 1800s. For more about *Homo economicus*, see Persky, 1995.

26 *Bernard de Mandeville, a Dutch doctor practising in England, published his famous book* The Fable of the Bees *in 1714*: see Mandeville, 1997.

27 *'America makes no sense without a deeply help faith – and I don't care what it is,' said President Dwight D. Eisenhower*: quoted in Nelson, 2002, p. 301.

CHAPTER THREE

29 *In women, lust and greed has always been criticized more harshly than it has in men*: see Folbre, 2010.

29 *'People call me a feminist whenever I express sentiments that differentiate me from a doormat or a prostitute,' wrote Rebecca West*: see West, 1989, p. 219.

30 *So they also didn't contribute to prosperity, thought economists in the 1800s*: the English economist Nassau Senior (1790–1864) was a key figure in this. See, for example, Senior, 1965.

31 *All human activity could be analysed using economic models*: see, for example, Becker, 1978.

31 *In 1979 the French philosopher Michel Foucault held a series of lectures at Collège de France in Paris*: see Foucault, 2010.

32 *To say that they 'are not feminist in their orientation would be as much of an understatement as to say that Bengal tigers are not vegetarians'*: quoted in Hewitson, 1999, p. 130.

33 *The Chicago economists started to ask completely new questions using the same economic logic,* the discussion of Gary Becker and the Chicago school in this chapter builds on Hewitson, 1999, pp. 37–64

33 *Women's lower wages were a result of women being less productive, the Chicago economists concluded*: see Mincer and Polachek, 1992. Jacob Mincer was indeed active at Columbia for most of his life, but is mostly associated with the Chicago School, mainly for his theories about human capital. He used them to describe wage differences before Gary Becker and T. W. Schultz.

34 *Therefore women invested less in their careers and therefore*

were paid less: this is a theory of human capital introduced by Jacob Mincer.

34 *But when the theories were compared with reality, it was clear that the explanations weren't sound*: see Hewitson, 1999, p. 50.

34 *Gary Becker's theory about racial discrimination is their best-known attempt*: see Becker, 1957.

35 *The problem was that it didn't turn out as the economists had expected*: see Arrow, 1972; Mueser, 1987.

35 *What does a married woman do when she comes home from work?*: see Becker, 1995.

36 *If they wrote anything at all, they stated briefly that it had to do with biology*: see, for example, Becker, 1991, p. 37.

37 *Sigmund Freud did indeed assert that women were inherently better at cleaning*: see Kipnis, 2006, pp. 81–122.

37 *A woman's sexual organ is an elegant self-regulated system – much cleaner than, for example, our mouths*: see Angier, 2000, p. 58.

CHAPTER FOUR

42 *'Economics is about money and why it is good,' said Woody Allen*: quoted in Brockway, 1996, p. 10.

42 *The British economist John Maynard Keynes once calculated*: for the argument that follows, see Keynes, 1931.

43 *Interest on interest, and a century later no one would have to go hungry again*: if output and consumption per capita grow at a rate of 2% each year, they will double approximately every thirty-five years. Within a century (103.5 years) consumption and income will increase eight-fold. After another thirty-five years they will have expanded sixteen times.

44 *'There are people in the world so hungry, that God cannot appear to them except in the form of bread'*: quoted in Marglin, 2008, p. 4.

44 *'One of those semi-criminal, semi-pathological propensities which one hands over with a shudder to the specialists in mental disease'*: see Keynes, 1963, p. 374.

45 *A middle class that has grown from 174 million to 806 million people in fifteen years*: follow the numbers at http://data.worldbank.org/country/china.

46 *The value of a life can be calculated like the value of a company, and now it's time to shut the doors*: Hamermesh and Soss, 1974.

46 *To faked orgasms*: see Mialon, 2012.

46 *Galenson has developed a statistical method to calculate which works of art are meaningful*: see Galenson, 2006.

47 *It's one thing to discuss what makes a work of art economically valuable: why one work is worth 12 million and another 100 million:* see, for example, Thompson, 2008.

47 *'We all want to believe that there is something special about the arts, but I don't buy that there is a difference between artistic and economic value'*: quoted in the *New York Times*, 4 August 2008.

48 *Then we land at about 11,000 dollars per person and no one has to go hungry again*: see, for example, CIA, *The World Fact Book*, http://www.cia.gov

48 *Every year approximately half a million women die in childbirth*: statistics from the United Nations Population Fund (UNFPA), http://www.unfpa.org

49 *The economist Amartya Sen calculated that if women had received equal care and nourishment, there would be*

100 million more women on earth: see Sen, 1990.

49   *70% of the world's poor are women*: statistic from the UN, http://www.un.org

49   *Where 1% of the USA's population alone earns a quarter of the cumulative income*: see Stiglitz, 2011.

49   *A wealthy American state like California spends more money on prisons than on universities*: see Center on Juvenile and Criminal Justice, 1996.

50   *'Just between you and me,' wrote Summers*: memo as quoted in the *Economist*, 8 February 1992.

52   *Imagine, the economists say, that Kenya isn't a country, but an individual*: for further discussion of the Summers memo, see Marglin, 2008.

53   *'Your reasoning is perfectly logical but completely insane'*: quoted in Jensen, 2002, p. 124.

53   *The region around the town of Guiyu in China is another*: see Walsh, 2009.

CHAPTER FIVE

56   *'I have the biggest cock in the building'*: quoted in Kipnis, 2006, p. 34.

56   *We're starting to become the men we used to want to marry*: the expression is usually attributed to the American feminist Gloria Steinem and has often been used by her.

57   *In certain countries this number reaches between 80 and 90%*: see Barker and Feiner, 2004, p. 123.

57   *The working hours of domestic labourers around the world are among the longest, the most precarious and the most unpredictable of any jobs on the labour market. Many women aren't allowed to leave the house without permission,*

according to a study conducted by Human Rights Watch: see Varia, 2007.

58 *The other is that a Filipina housekeeper in Hong Kong earns as much money as a male doctor in the rural Philippines*: see Hochschild, 2000.

58 *The money that female migrants send home contributes more to the economy of many countries than aid and foreign investments combined*: see Kingma, 2007.

59 *The young woman in the Lowveld in Zimbabwe wakes up at 4 a.m. to carry a bucket eleven kilometres to the well and back*: see Waring, 1999.

60 *The equivalent statistic for men is one quarter*: see *Human Development Report*, 1999, p. 78.

60 *Because no one had bothered to quantify housework, we might have overvalued the actual increase of wealth*: for further discussion of this topic, see Folbre, 2002, p. 67.

61 *Between 30.6 and 41.4% of the GDP, they concluded*; see, for example, Hamdad, 2003.

62 *You can't just add women and stir,* this expression is used by Australian feminist economist Gillian J. Hewitson to describe the strategy of incorporating women into an existing discipline rather than to change it. See Hewitson, 1999, p. 37

62 *In 1957 Betty Friedan, then a thirty-six-year-old mother of two, sent out a questionnaire to her former classmates*: for more on Friedan's life, see Hennessee, 1999.

63 *'Pulled the trigger on history'*: quoted in Fox, 2006.

65 *Studies show that since the 1970s women in the West have felt that they have become less happy*: see Stevenson and Wolfers, 2009.

65 *In Britain you find little difference between men's and women's happiness. The exception here is divorced fathers*: see Office for National Statistics, 2012b

CHAPTER SIX

69 *A zero-sum game between two participants*: see, for example, Leonard, 2010.

71 *And the necessity of producing the unusual or facing extinction*: see Poundstone, 1992, p. 66.

71 *and the ultimate distance at which people would be killed*: see Rhodes, 1987, p. 628.

73 *We must look at the factors that make war predictable, whatever the context*: see Aumann, 2005. http://www.nobelprize.org/nobel_prizes/economic-sciences/laureates/2005/aumann-lecture.pdf

73 *Dr Strangelove*: John von Neumann is said to have been a model for Stanley Kubrick's Dr Strangelove in the 1964 comedy *Dr. Strangelove or: How I Learned to Stop Worrying and Love the Bomb*.

74 *In the same way that physicists formulated laws for matter and energy, finance tried to formulate laws for stocks and derivatives*: see, for example, Taylor, 2004, pp. 142–72.

74 *'Think how hard physics would be if the electrons could think'*: Murray Gell-Mann quoted in Grazzini, 2009, p. 2.

75 *'The game is much bigger and much more interesting to me than casino gambling,' said Edward Thorp*: quoted in Taylor 2004, p. 174.

76 *Theologians have compared the efficient market hypothesis to the word of God*: see Taylor 2004, p. 244–48.

78 *The efficient market hypothesis has been called 'the biggest*

mistake in the history of finance': the statement is sometimes credited to Larry Summers and sometimes to Robert Shiller; see, for example, Jeremy Grantham's foreword to Smithers, 2009.

78　*The financier George Soros suggests it's the opposite*: see Soros, 1994.

CHAPTER SEVEN

80　*What can the second act of Johann Wolfgang von Goethe's great drama* Faust *teach us about economics?*: for more on the economic themes in *Faust*, see Binswanger, 1994.

81　*The history of money is a journey from the material to the immaterial*: for a more detailed argument, see, for example, Weatherford, 1998.

85　*In 1997 rock legend David Bowie needed money*: see Buckley, 2000, pp. 536–38.

88　*This was the biggest economic bubble in the history of mankind*: see the *Economist*, 2005.

89　*Speculation arises when our collective fantasy locks its sights on something that we think is completely new and unique*: see Galbraith, 1994, p. 28.

89　*When it becomes known that people are earning a lot of money in a certain market, more people invest there*: for a rationale of bubbles, see Kindleberger, 2000.

90　*'The illusion has become real. And the more real it becomes, the more desperately they want it'*: Gordon Gekko in the 1987 film *Wall Street*.

90　*Today abstract algorithms are increasingly replacing the broker's contribution to the financial markets*: see Grant and Mackenzie, 2010.

92 *When the crisis became a fact in the autumn of 2008, Alan Greenspan, chief of the American Federal Reserve, was inter-rogated in Congress*: the testimony is available to read at http://www.pbs.org. In the meantime, Greenspan hasn't let go of his ideology. In the *Financial Times* in 29 March 2011, he wrote, 'Today's competitive markets, whether we seek to recognize it or not, are driven by an international version of Adam Smith's "invisible hand" that is unredeemably opaque. With notably rare exceptions (2008, for example), the global "invisible hand" has created relatively stable exchange rates, interest rates, prices, and wage rates.'

CHAPTER EIGHT

94 *The first full-frontal attack on economic man was published in 1979*: Kahneman and Tversky, 1979.

94 *Kahneman was awarded the 2002 Nobel Prize in Economic Sciences*: Tversky died in 1996, otherwise he would have also been awarded it.

95 *It also matters if people bargain with each other face to face*: for these arguments, see chapter two in Smith, 2000, as well as Aktipis and Kurzban in Koppl, 2005.

96 *Economic behaviour is in many ways driven by emotion – not by reason. And it is collective – not individualist*: see Akerlof and Shiller, 2009.

97 *Psychologists conducted an experiment with nursery school children and with students in the second and sixth grades to see if they were like economic man*: see Bereby-Meyer and Fisk, 2009.

98 *The economist and philosopher Amartya Sen has illustrated this with the following exchange*: see Sen, 1990, p. 35.

98 *The neoliberal economist Milton Friedman's famous challenge to this kind of criticism is about billiards*: see Friedman, 1953.

99 *John Kenneth Galbraith once quipped that God created economists to give astrologists a better reputation*: in *US News and World Report*, 7 March 1988, p. 64, but it is not certain that it can indeed be attributed to Galbraith.

99 *The Nobel-prize-winning American economist Robert Lucas felt compelled to answer the Queen*: see Lucas, 2009.

100 *The United States Department of the Treasury pushed through a privatization of Russia with record speed*: see Stiglitz, 2003, pp. 133–66.

101 *Making a capitalist economy communist is 'like making fish soup from an aquarium'*: from an article by Amanda Friedeman in the *Chicago Daily Observer*, 30 January 2010.

103 *You'd say he's mad*: for a rational explanation of mental illness, see Caplan, 2005.

CHAPTER NINE

106 *It was considered important to keep commerce outside the human community*: for more on this, see Taylor, 2009, p. 69.

108 *'With all the talk about how to stimulate it, you'd think that the economy is a giant clitoris'*: Ehrenreich, 2008.

112 *Two economists conducted a study of the problem*: Gneezy and Rustichini, 2000.

114 *Like when a charity started offering free vaccinations in rural India*: see Banerjee and Duflo, 2011, pp. 57–70.

114 *An economic study was done in Switzerland before the country held one of its many referendums*: see Schwartz, 2007.

CHAPTER TEN

116 Nancy Folbre, a feminist economics professor, often tells this tale: see Folbre, 2001 p. 22–23.

118 The one was done for money. The other out of thoughtfulness. And never the twain shall meet: for more on this dichotomy, see Folbre and Nelson, 2000.

118 'Money is human happiness in the abstract': in *Counsels and Maxims Vol. 2*, chapter twenty-six, §320, translated by T. Bailey Saunders.

120 The founder of the modern nursing profession, Florence Nightingale, was born in Florence in 1820 to British parents: the following discussion of Florence Nightingale expands on Moberg, 2007.

123 Around 3,500 Filipino doctors were retrained as nurses between 2000 and 2003: see Agence France-Presse, 2005.

124 In Sweden there is expected to be a deficit of 130,000 qualified care workers in 2030: the prognosis from the SCB (Statistics Sweden) refers to 130,000 graduates of healthcare programmes – enrolled nurses, nursing auxiliaries, etc. The reason is an increase in the elderly population, combined with a low interest in healthcare programmes. See *Trender och prognoser* [Trends and prognoses], 2008, http://www.scb.se

CHAPTER ELEVEN

126 In 1978 Deng Xiaoping began to liberalize the Chinese economy: the section on China is based on Leonard, 2008.

127 When fourteen employees in a sixteen-month period killed themselves at iPhone manufacturer Foxconn, salaries were raised by 30%: see Johnson, 2011.

129 'There is no such thing as society,' said Thatcher: quoted by

Douglas Keay in *Woman's Own*, 31 October 1987.

132 In 1974 economist Arthur Laffer, Wall Street Journal writer Jude Wanniski and one Dick Cheney met in a hotel room in Washington, DC: see Chait, 2007.

134 'By 1982, I knew the Reagan Revolution was impossible': see Stockman, 1986, p. 13.

134 The richest 0.1% of America's population tripled its share of the national revenue between 1978 and 1999: see Harvey, 2007, p. 16.

135 From 45 times the pay of the average employee in 1998 to 120 times in 2010: see Mount, 2012, p. 3.

135 J. K. Rowling, who wrote the Harry Potter books, earns an enormous amount more than Charles Dickens did in his time: see Cowen, 2011.

135 According to the UN, the world in 2005 was less equal than it was ten years before: see United Nations Publications, 2005.

135 One hundred years ago, the ratio was more like nine to one: see Rothkopf, 2008, p. 94.

136 On a similar German ranking of multi-million-euro plutocrats, only one in six was female: see Wolf, 2013, p. 141.

136 Women still only make up 9% of dollar-billionaires in the world: according to the 2009 *Forbes* list.

136 This pattern of female wealth equalling inherited wealth is so prominent that Lena Edlund and Wojciech Kopczuk of Columbia University have been able to show that the more wealth that is held by women, the more stagnant the economy is: see Edlund and Kopczuk, 2009.

136 In the 1980s, something called 'paper entrepreneurship' arose: the term was coined in Reich, 1983.

136 In 2008, 41% of Harvard Business School graduates went on to work with hedge funds, investment banks and capital risk companies: according to the so-called Harvard MBA Indicator from 2009, which is compiled by Soifer Consulting.

137 During the era that preceded the crisis of the 1930s, the division of wealth in the USA was almost identical to what it was before the financial crisis of 2008: see Krugman, 2000.

137 'God is with everybody ... and in the long run, he plumps for the people who have the most money and the biggest armies': From Anouilh's play *The Lark*.

CHAPTER TWELVE

139 The world's tallest building is in Dubai: for the section on Dubai, see Davis and Monk, 2007.

140 The neoliberal ideology does not in fact conceive of the market as something 'natural': see Brown, 2008.

142 The French philosopher Michel Foucault thought that liberalism and neoliberalism distinguished themselves from each other in how they perceived economic activity: see Foucault, 2010.

143 'Economics are the method; the object is to change the heart and soul': from an interview with Ronald Butt in the *Sunday Times*, 3 May 1981.

143 For Karl Marx, the development of capital was a process through which workers' knowledge, skill and humanity was mechanized bit by bit: the discussion about alienation and human capital is based on Read, 2009.

145 The Chicago economists found the term 'human capital' in Smith and included it in their theories: see Mincer, 1958.

145 *'It may seem odd now, but I hesitated a while before deciding to call my book* Human Capital: Becker, 1992, p. 43.

146 *The conflict Marx spoke of dissolves, but not in the way he imagined*: see Lemke, 2001.

CHAPTER THIRTEEN

148 *The mother doesn't exist. She has become a void – the already autonomous tiny space hero flies forth*: the discussion of individualism and Lennart Nilsson's pictures builds on Newman, 1996.

152 *Behavioural economics, the school that has made the biggest impact in recent years*: for more on behavioural economics see Östling, 2009.

154 *The word 'individual' means, precisely, indivisible*: see Franklin, 1991.

155 *The natural human state is to be enveloped by our dependency on others*: see Held, 1990.

156 *What's interesting is that we so dearly want him to align with reality*: this is formulated from another perspective and with different conclusions in Feiner, 2003.

CHAPTER FOURTEEN

157 *In the 1500s and 1600s, the relationship between man and nature changed in the West*: for more about the views of sex and gender that the discussion in this chapter builds on, see, for example, Hewitson, 1999, pp. 108–38.

160 *'No discrimination exists if pregnant men and pregnant women are treated the same'*: quoted in Graycar and Morgan, 1990.

162 *'You sought a flower and found a fruit. You sought a spring*

and found a sea. You sought a woman and found a soul – you are disappointed': From Edith Södergran's poem 'The Day Cools', 1916.

163 *Economic man's parodically simple behaviour doesn't mean that he isn't conjured from deep inner conflicts*: see also Feiner, 1999.

CHAPTER FIFTEEN

170 *In one of her poems, Muriel Rukeyser revisits the Greek myth of King Oedipus*: quoted as an epigraph in Folbre, 2010.

175 *The founders of economic science viewed the field in explicitly messianic terms*: see Nelson, 1993.

178 *On noticing that roses smell better than cabbage, you can't conclude that they will make better soup*: Mencken, 2006, p. 19.

CHAPTER SIXTEEN

180 *After the crash Icelandic banks lost 100 billion dollars*: see Lewis, 2009.

182 *In Lao Tzu's classical work* Tao Te Ching, *written in China in around 600 BC, yin and yang's movements beget each other*: for more about Lao Tzu and feminism, see Chuan Xu, 2003.

183 *The most famous definition of economics was made by Lionel Robbins in 1932*: see Robbins, p. 16.

183 *How different the world would be, the economist Julie Nelson muses*: see Ferber and Nelson, 1993, p. 26.

188 *Why are you unhappy? wrote the poet Wei Wu Wei*: from *Ask The Awakened; The Negative Way*, Sentient Publications, 2003.

EPILOGUE

193 For men, that figure is one per cent: figures from the Equality and Human Rights Commission (EHRC) suggest that 17 per cent of unemployed women left their last job to care for someone, compared with only 1 per cent of men (Smeaton et al 2009). This disparity is particularly acute for low-income older women.

195 When women are forced to choose between a career and children, many women choose the career: there are exceptions – Ireland still has Europe's highest birth rate, while practising a very traditional family policy.

BIBLIOGRAPHY

Agence France-Presse, 'Warnings Raised About Exodus of Philippine Doctors and Nurses', *New York Times*, 27 November 2005.

Akerlof, George A. and Shiller, Robert J., *Animal Spirits: How Human Psychology Drives the Economy, and Why It Matters for Global Capitalism*, Princeton University Press, 2009.

Aktipis, Athena C. and Kurzban, Robert O., *Is Homo Economicus Extinct?*, in R. Koppl, *Evolutionary Psychology and Economic Theory*, JAI Press, 2005.

Angier, Natalie, *Woman: An Intimate Geography*, Anchor, 2000.

Arrow, Kenneth J., *Models of Job Discrimination*, in A. H. Pascal, *Racial Discrimination in Economic Life*, Lexington Books, 1972.

Aumann, Robert J., *War and Peace*, Nobel lecture, 8 December 2005, http:/www.nobelprize.org

Banerjee, Abhijit and Duflo, Esther, *Poor Economics: A Radical Rethinking of the Way to Fight Global Poverty*, Public Affairs Books, 2011.

Barker, Drucilla K. and Feiner, Susan F., *Liberating Economics: Feminist Perspectives on Families, Work and Globalization*, University of Michigan Press, 2004.

Bebchuk, Lucian, A., Cohen, Alma and Spamann, Holger, 'The Wages of Failure: Executive Compensation at Bear Stearns and Lehman 2000–2008', *Yale Journal on Regulation*, vol. 27, 2010.

Becker, Gary S., *A Treatise on the Family*, Harvard University Press, 1991.

Becker, Gary S., 'Human Capital, Effort and the Sexual Division of Labor', in J. Humphries, ed., *Gender and Economics*, Edward Elgar Publishing, 1995.

Becker, Gary S., *The Economic Approach to Human Behavior*, University of Chicago Press, 1978.

Becker, Gary S., *The Economics of Discrimination*, University of Chicago Press, 1957.

Becker, Gary S., *The Economic Way of Looking at Life*, Nobel lecture, 9 December 1992, http://home.uchicago.edu/gbecker/Nobel/nobellecture.pdf

Bereby-Meyer, Yoella and Fisk, Shelly, *Is Homo Economicus a Five-Year-Old?*, Ben Gurion University of the Negev, 2009.

Binswanger, Hans Christoph, *Money and Magic: A Critique of the Modern Economy in the Light of Goethe's Faust*, University of Chicago Press, 1994.

Booth, Alison, Cardona-Sosac, Lina and Nolena, Patrick: 'Gender Differences in Risk Aversion: Do Single-Sex Environments Affect Their Development?' *Journal of Economic Behavior and Organization*, vol. 99, pp. 126–54, March 2014.

Brockway, George P., *The End of Economic Man: Principles of Any Future Economics*, W. W. Norton & Company, 1996.

Brown, Wendy, *Att vinna framtiden åter*, Atlas, 2008.

Buckley, David, *Strange Fascination – David Bowie: The Definitive Story*, Virgin Books, 2000.

Caplan, Bryan, *The Economics of Szasz: Preferences, Constraints, and Mental Illness*, Department of Economics, Center for Study of Public Choice and Mercatus Center, George Mason University, 2005.

Center on Juvenile and Criminal Justice, *From Classrooms Cell Blocks*, October 1996, http://www.cjcj.org

Chait, Jonathan, *The Big Con: The True Story of How Washington Got Hoodwinked and Hijacked by Crackpot Economics*, Houghton Mifflin Harcourt, 2007.

Chuan Xu, Judith, 'Poststructuralist Feminism and the Problem of Femininity in the Daodejing', *Journal of Feminist Studies in Religion*, vol. 19, no. 1, 2003.

Cohen, Patricia, 'A Textbook Example of Ranking Artworks', *New York Times*, 4 August 2008.

Cowen, Tyler, 'The Inequality that Matters', *American Interest*, January/February 2011.

Croson, Rachel and Uri, Gneezy: 'Gender Differences in Preferences', *Journal of Economic Literature* 47(2): pp. 448–74, 2009.

Davis, John B., *The Theory of the Individual in Economics: Identity and Value*, Routledge, 2003.

Davis, Mike and Monk, Daniel Bertrand, *Evil Paradises: Dreamworlds of Neoliberalism*, New Press, 2007.

de Beauvoir, Simone, *The Second Sex*, Norstedts, 2006.

Defoe, Daniel, *Robinson Crusoe*, Wordsworth Editions, 1992.

Edgeworth, F. Y., *Mathematical Physics, An Essay on the Application of Mathematics to the Moral Sciences*, Reprints of Economic Classics, Augustus M. Kelley Publishers, 1967 (1881).

Edlund, L. and Kopczuk, W., 'Women, wealth and mobility'. American Economic Review, 99 (1) (2009), pp. 146–78.

Ehrenreich, Barbara, 'Clitoral Economics', *Huffington Post*, 22 January 2008.

Feiner, Susan F., 'Portrait of *Homo Economicus* as a Young Man', in Mark Osteen and Martha Woodmansee, *The New Economic Criticism: Studies at the Intersection of Literature and Economics*, Routledge, 1999.

Feiner, Susan F., 'Reading Neoclassical Economics: Toward an Erotic Economy of Sharing', in Drucilla K. Barker and

Edith Kuiper, *Toward a Feminist Philosophy of Economics*, Routledge, 2003.

Ferber, Marianne A. and Nelson, Julie, *Beyond Economic Man: Feminist Theory and Economics*, Chicago University Press, 1993.

Folbre, Nancy, *Greed, Lust and Gender: A History of Economic Ideas*, Oxford University Press, 2010.

Folbre, Nancy, *The Invisible Heart: Economics and Family Values*, New Press, 2001.

Folbre, Nancy and Nelson, Julie A., 'For Love or Money – Or Both?', *Journal of Economic Perspectives*, vol. 14, no. 4, 2000.

Foucault, Michel, 'The Birth of Biopolitics', in *Michel Foucault: Lectures at the Collège de France*, Palgrave, 2010.

Fox, Margalit, 'Betty Friedan, Who Ignited Cause in "Feminine Mystique", Dies at 85', *New York Times*, 5 February 2006.

Franklin, Sarah, 'Fetal Fascinations: New Dimensions to the Medical-Scientific Construction of Fetal Personhood', in S. Franklin, C. Lury & J. Stacey, *Off Centre: Feminism and Cultural Studies*, HarperCollins Academic, 1991.

Frey, Bruno, *Not Just for the Money: An Economic Theory of Personal Motivation*, Edward Elgar Publishing, 1997.

Friedan, Betty, *The Feminine Mystique*, trans. Gun Trollbäck, Pan/Norstedts, 1968.

Friedman, Milton, 'The Methodology of Positive Economics', in *Essays in Positive Economics*, University of Chicago Press, 1953.

Galbraith, John Kenneth, *A Short History of Financial Euphoria*, Penguin, 1994.

Galenson, David W., *Artistic Capital*, Routledge, 2006.

Gilder, George, *Wealth and Poverty*, ICS Press, 1993.

Gneezy, Uri and Rustichini, Aldo, 'A Fine is a Price', *Journal of Legal Studies*, vol. 29, no. 1, January 2000.

Grant, Jeremy and Mackenzie, Michael, 'Ghosts in the Machine: The Potential Dangers of Automated, High-Frequency Trading', *Financial Times*, 17 February 2010.

Grant Thornton International Business Report (IBR) 2012, 'Women in Senior Management: Still Not Enough', 2012.

Grapard, Ulla and Hewitson, Gillian, *Robinson Crusoe's Economic Man*, Routledge, 2011.

Graycar, Regina and Morgan, Jenny, *The Hidden Gender of Law*, Federation Press, 1990.

Grazzini, Jakob, 'The Rhetoric of Economics by D. N. McCloskey', University of Turin Doctoral Programme in Economics of Complexity and Creativity, 2009.

Hamdad, Malika, 'Valuing Households' Unpaid Work in Canada, 1992 and 1998: Trends and Sources of Change', Statistics Canada Economic Conference, 2003.

Hammermesh, Daniel S. and Soss, Neal M., 'An Economic Theory of Suicide', *Journal of Political Economy*, 82, January/February 1974.

Harvey, David, *A Brief History of Neoliberalism*, Oxford University Press, 2007.

Hawking, Stephen, *Black Holes and Baby Universes and Other Essays*, Bantam Books, 1993.

Held, Virginia, *Mothering Versus Contract*, in Jane J. Mansbridge, *Beyond Self-Interest*, University of Chicago Press, 1990.

Hennessee, Judith, *Betty Friedan: Her Life*, Random House, 1999.

Hewitson, Gillian 'Deconstructing Robinson Crusoe: A Feminist Interrogation of "Rational Economic Man"', *Australian Feminist Studies*, vol. 9, issue 20, pp. 131–49, 1994.

Hewitson, Gillian, *Feminist Economics*, Edward Elgar Publishing, 1999.

Hochschild, Arlie Russell and Ehrenreich, Barbara, eds., *Global*

Woman: Nannies, Maids and Sex Workers in the New Economy, Henry Holt, 2002.

Human Development Report 1999, United Nations Development Programme, 1999.

Jensen, Derrick, *The Culture of Make Believe*, Context Books, 2002.

Johnson, Joel, '1 Million Workers. 90 Million iPhones. 17 Suicides. Who's to Blame?', *Wired Magazine*, March 2011.

Joyce, James, *Daniel Defoe*, Buffalo Studies 1, 1964.

Kahneman, Daniel and Tversky, Amos, 'Prospect Theory: An Analysis of Decision under Risk', *Econometrica*, XLVII, 1979.

Keynes, John Maynard, *Essays in Persuasion*, W. W. Norton & Company, 1963.

Kindleberger, Charles P., and Aliber, Robert Z., *Manias, Panics, and Crashes: A History of Financial Crises*, Wiley Investment Classics, 2000.

Kingma, Mireille, 'Nurses on the Move: A Global Overview', in *Health Services Research*, vol. 42, no. 3, p. 2, 2007.

Kipnis, Laura, *The Female Thing*, Pantheon Books, 2006.

Krugman, Paul, *The Return of Depression Economics*, W. W. Norton & Company, 2000.

Lagarde, Christine, 'Women, Power and the Challenge of the Financial Crisis', *International Herald Tribune*, 10 May 2010.

Lemke, Thomas, 'The Birth of Biopolitics: Michel Foucault's Lecture at the Collège de France on Neo-Liberal Governmentality', in *Economy and Society*, vol. 30, no. 2, May 2001.

Leonard, Mark, *What Does China Think?*, Fourth Estate, 2008.

Leonard, Robert, *Von Neumann, Morgenstern and the Creation of Game Theory*, Cambridge University Press, 2010.

Levitt, Steven D. and Dubner, Stephen J., *Freakonomics: A Rogue Economist Explores the Hidden Side of Everything*, William Morrow, 2006.

Lewis, Michael, 'Wall Street on the Tundra', *Vanity Fair*, 14 December 2009.

Lucas, Robert, 'In Defence of the Dismal Science', *Economist*, 6 August 2009.

Mandeville, Bernard, *The Fable of the Bees and Other Writings*, Hackett Publishing, 1997.

Marglin, Stephen A., *The Dismal Science: How Thinking Like an Economist Undermines Community*, Harvard University Press, 2008.

Marshall, Alfred, *Principles of Economics*, Macmillan and Co., 1920.

McCloskey, Deirdre, *How to be Human*: *Though an Economist*, University of Michigan Press, 2000.

McCloskey, Deirdre, *If You're So Smart: The Narrative of Economic Expertise*, University of Chicago Press, 1992.

Mencken, H. L., *A Little Book in C Major*, Kessinger Publishing, 2006.

Mialon, Hugo, 'The Economics of Faking Ecstasy', *Economic Inquiry*, vol. 50, no. 1, January 2012.

Milne, A. A., *If I May*, Kessinger Publishing, 2004.

Mincer, Jacob, 'Investment in Human Capital and Personal Income Distribution', *Journal of Political Economy*, vol. 66, no. 4, August 1958.

Mincer, Jacob and Polachek, Solomon, 'Family Investment in Human Capital: Earnings of Women', in *Studies in Labor Supply: Collected Essays of Jacob Mincer*, vol. 2, Edward Elgar Publishing, 1992.

Moberg, Åsa, *Hon var ingen Florence Nightingale: människan bakom myten* [She was no Florence Nightingale: the person behind the myth], Natur & Kultur, 2007.

Mount, Ferdinand, *The New Few, or a Very British Oligarchy: Power and Inequality in Britain Now*, Simon & Schuster, 2012.

Mueser, Peter, 'Discrimination', in John Eatwell and Murray Milgate, *The New Palgrave: A Dictionary in Economics*, vol. 1, Stockton, 1987.

Nelson, Robert H., *Economics As Religion: From Samuelson to Chicago and Beyond*, Pennsylvania State University, 2002.

Nelson, Robert H., *Reaching for Heaven on Earth: The Theological Meaning of Economics*, Rowman & Littlefield Publishers, 1993.

Newman, Karen, *Fetal Positions: Individualism, Science, Visuality*, Stanford University Press, 1996.

Office for National Statistics (ONS). First ONS Annual Experimental Subjective Well-being Results. Swansea: ONS, 2012b.

Östling, Robert, *Beteendeekonomi och konsumentpolitik* [Behavioural Economics and Consumer Politics], Integrations och Jämställdhetsdepartementet, 2009.

Pateman, Carole, 'The Patriarchal Welfare State', in Joan Landes, ed., *Feminism, the Public and the Private: Oxford Readings in Feminism*, Oxford University Press, 1998.

Pearson, Matthew and Schipper, Burkhard, 'Menstrual Cycle and Competitive Bidding', *Games and Economic Behavior*, vol. 78, pp. 1–20, March 2013.

Persky, Joseph, 'Retrospectives: The Ethology of *Homo Economicus*', *Journal of Economic Perspectives*, vol. 9, no. 2, 1995.

Phillipson, Nicholas, *Adam Smith: An Enlightened Life*, Yale University Press, 2010.

Poundstone, William, *Prisoner's Dilemma: John von Neumann, Game Theory, and the Puzzle of the Bomb*, Oxford University Press, 1992.

Read, Jason, *A Genealogy of Homo Economicus: Neoliberalism and the Production of Subjectivity*, Foucault Studies, no. 6, 2009.

Reich, Robert B., *The Next American Frontier*, Crown, 1983.

Reinhart, Carmen M. and Rogoff, Kenneth S., *This Time Is*

Different: Eight Centuries of Financial Folly, Princeton University Press, 2011.

Rhodes, Richard, *The Making of the Atomic Bomb*, Simon & Schuster, 1987.

Robbins, Lionel, *An Essay on the Nature and Significance of Economic Science*, second edition, revised, Macmillan & Co, 1945.

Rothkopf, David, *Superclass: The Global Power Elite and the World They Are Making*, Leopard Förlag, 2008.

Schwartz, Barry, 'Money for Nothing', *New York Times*, 2 July 2007.

Sen, Amartya, 'More than 100 Million Women are Missing', *New York Review of Books*, 20 December 1990.

Sen, Amartya, 'Rational Fools: A Critique of the Behavioral Foundations of Economic Theory', in Jane J. Manbridge, *Beyond Self-Interest*, University of Chicago Press, 1990.

Senior, Nassau, *An outline of the Science of Political Economy*, Augustus M. Kelley, 1965.

Simmel, Georg, *The Philosophy of Money*, Routledge, 2004.

Smeaton D., Vergeris S. and Sahin-Dikmen M., *Older Workers: Employment Preferences, Barriers and Solutions*, Equality and Human Rights Commission, Research report 43, 2009

Smith, Adam, *The Wealth of Nations*, Encyclopædia Britannica, Great Books, 1952 (1759).

Smith, Vernon L., *Bargaining and Market Behavior: Essays in Experimental Economics*, Cambridge University Press, 2000.

Smithers, Andrew, *Wall Street Revalued: Imperfect Markets and Inept Central Bankers*, John Wiley & Sons, 2009.

Soros, George, *The Alchemy of Finance: Reading the Mind of the Market*, Wiley, 1994.

'Special Report on the Global Housing Boom', *Economist*, 18 June 2005.

Statistics Sweden, 'Pay Differentials between Women and Men in Sweden', *Information on Education and the Labour market 2004: 2.*

Stevenson, Betsey and Wolfers, Justin, 'The Paradox of Declining Female Happiness', *American Economic Journal: Economic Policy* 2009, vol. 1, no. 2, pp. 190225.

Stigler, G. J., 'Smith's Travels on the Ship of State', *History of Political Economy*, vol. 3, no. 2, 1971.

Stiglitz, Joseph E., *Globalization and Its Discontents*, W. W. Norton & Company, 2003.

Stiglitz, Joseph E., 'Of the 1%, By the 1%, For the 1%', *Vanity Fair*, May 2011.

Stockman, David, *The Triumph of Politics: Why the Reagan Revolution Failed*, Harper & Row, 1986.

Szuchman, Paula and Anderson, Jenny, *Spousonomics: Using Economics to Master Love, Marriage, and Dirty Dishes*, Random House, 2011.

Taylor, Mark C., *Confidence Games: Money and Markets in a World without Redemption*, University of Chicago Press, 2008.

Thompson, Don, *The $12 Million Stuffed Shark: The Curious Economics of Contemporary Art*, Palgrave Macmillan, 2008.

Thorp, Edward O., *Beat the Dealer: A Winning Strategy for the Game of Twenty-One*, Vintage, 1966.

Thorp, Edward O., *Beat the Market: A Scientific Stock Market System*, Random House, 1967.

United Nations Publications, *The Inequality Predicament: Report on the World Social Situation*, Department of Economic and Social Affairs (DESA), 2005.

Varia, Nisha, 'Globalization Comes Home: Protecting Migrant Domestic Workers' Rights', Human Rights Watch World Report 2007, http://www.hrw.org

Walsh, Bryan, 'E-Waste Not', *TIME* magazine, 8 January 2009.

Wanniski, Jude, *The Way the World Works*, Gateway Editions, 1998.

Waring, Marilyn, *Counting for Nothing: What Men Value and What Women are Worth*, University of Toronto Press, 1999.

Weatherford, Jack, *The History of Money*, Three Rivers Press, 1998.

West, Rebecca, *The Young Rebecca: Writings of Rebecca West, 1911–17*, a selection made by Jane Marcus, Indiana University Press, 1989.

Wolf, Alison, *The XX Factor: How Working Women Are Creating A New Society*, Profile Books, 2013

CREDITS

INDEX OF PERSONS

Aiello, Carolyn 160
Akerlof, George 96, 209, 217
Allen, Woody 42, 203
Anderson, Jenny 109, 110, 226
Anouilh, Jean 137, 213
Aristotle 84
Astaire, Fred 66
Aumann, Robert 207, 217
Becker, Gary 31, 32, 34, 35, 40, 145, 202, 203, 214, 218
Beckham, David 139
Bergmann, Barbara 32
Borg, Anders 108
Bowie, David 85, 86, 87, 208, 218
Brown, Wendy 140, 218
Bush Sr., George 132
Calvin, John 85
Castro, Fidel 15
Cheney, Dick 132, 133, 212
Clinton, Bill 50
de Beauvoir, Simone 16, 200, 219
Defoe, Daniel 18, 19, 201, 219, 222
Defries, Tony 85
Deng Xiaoping 126, 127, 128, 212
Dickens, Charles 135, 212
Drake, Francis 42, 43
Ehrenreich, Barbara 108, 210, 219, 221
Einstein, Albert 14, 174
Eisenhower, Dwight D. 27, 210
Elizabeth I, Queen of England 42
Elizabeth II, Queen 99, 210
Folbre, Nancy 116, 201, 202, 206, 211, 215, 220
Foucault, Michel 31, 32, 142, 143,

145, 146, 152, 202, 213, 220, 225
Fredrik III, Emperor of Germany 71
Freud, Sigmund 37, 38, 203
Friedan, Betty 62, 63, 66, 206, 220, 221
Friedman, Milton 31, 98, 99, 129, 139, 210, 220
Galbraith, John Kenneth 99, 208, 210, 220
Galenson, David 46, 47, 204, 220
Gandhi, Mahatma 44, 180
Geduldig, Dwight 160
Gell-Mann, Murray 74, 207
Gere, Richard 162
Gilder, George 132, 133, 220
von Goethe, Johann Wolfgang 80, 81, 90, 208, 218
Gray, Charles 47
Greenspan, Alan 92, 209
Hayek, Friedrich 129
Held, Virginia 155, 221
Homer 181
Johnson, Lyndon B. 150
Joyce, James 21, 201, 222
Kahneman, Daniel 94, 151, 209, 222
Keynes, John Maynard 42, 43, 44, 45, 46, 47, 48, 49, 50, 54, 55, 96, 97, 131, 203, 204, 222
Laffer, Arthur 132, 133, 134, 212
Lao Tzu 182, 215
Lucas, Robert 99, 210, 223
Luther, Martin 174
Lutzenberger, José 53
Madoff, Bernard 175
Mandeville, Bernard 26, 201, 223

229

Mao Zedong 126, 127

Marx, Karl 27, 143, 144, 146, 191, 214

Mencken, H. L. 177, 215, 223

Merton, Robert C. 100

Milne, A. A. 18, 201, 223

Morgan, J. P. 135

Morgenstern, Oskar 70, 71, 222

Nelson, Julie 183, 211, 216, 220

Nelson, Robert H. 174, 175, 176, 177, 202, 215, 224

von Neumann, John 69, 70, 71, 72, 73, 74, 207, 222, 224

Newton, Isaac 11, 12, 14, 154, 174, 199

Nightingale, Florence 120, 121, 122, 123, 193, 211, 223, 224

Nilsson, Lennart 148, 149, 150, 151, 214

Obama, Barack 50

Oliver, Jamie 158

Picasso, Pablo 47

Putin, Vladimir 101

Reagan, Ronald 128, 129, 130, 131, 132, 134, 212, 226

Regan, Judith 56

Reinhart, Carmen M. 89, 225

Robbins, Lionel 14, 183, 200, 216, 225

Roberts, Julia 162

Rogers, Ginger 66

Rogoff, Kenneth S. 89, 225

Rowling, J. K. 135, 212

Rukeyser, Muriel 170, 215

Scholes, Myron 100

Schopenhauer, Arthur 118

Sen, Amartya 49, 98, 204, 210, 225

Shakespeare, William 159

Shiller, Robert 96, 208, 209, 217

Simmel, Georg 81, 225

Smith, Adam 8, 9, 10, 11, 12, 14, 15, 16, 17, 26, 27, 40, 41, 44, 70, 76, 117, 118, 125, 141, 142, 143, 144, 145, 146, 172, 186, 190, 191, 197, 199, 201, 209, 214, 224

Soros, George 78, 208, 226

Stigler, George J. 31, 199, 226

Stockman, David 134, 212, 226

Stone, Oliver 90

Summers, Lawrence 50, 51, 52, 53, 205, 208

Szuchman, Paula 109, 110, 226

Södergran, Edith 162, 215

Thales 84, 85

Thatcher, Margaret 15, 31, 128, 129, 130, 131, 143

Thomas Aquinas 174

Thorp, Edward 75, 207, 226

Toffler, Alvin 63

Tversky, Amos 94, 151, 209, 222

Verdi, Guiseppe 162

Volcker, Paul 128

Wałęsa, Lech 101

Wanniski, Jude 132, 133, 134, 212, 227

Waring, Marilyn 59, 200, 206, 227

Waxman, Henry 92

Wei Wu Wei 188, 216

West, Rebecca 29, 202, 227

Wilde, Oscar 106

Wolf, Naomi 66

Woolf, Virginia 1, 191